The Thames

Mortimer Menpes, G E. Mitton

THE THAMES

AGENTS

AMERICA . THE MACMILLAN COMPANY
64 & 66 FIFTH AVENUE, NEW YORK

CANADA . THE MACMILLAN COMPANY OF CANADA, LTD.
27 RICHMOND STREET, TORONTO

INDIA . . MACMILLAN & COMPANY, LTD.
MACMILLAN BUILDING, BOMBAY
309 BOW BAZAAR STREET, CALCUTTA

PUNTING

THE THAMES

BY MORTIMER MENPES, R.I.

TEXT BY G. E. MITTON

PUBLISHED BY A. & C. BLACK

SOHO SQUARE, LONDON, W.

Published July 1906

CONTENTS

CHAPTER XIV

CHAPTER XV

CHAPTER XVI

CHAPTER XVII

CHAPTER XVIII

CHAPTER XIX

LIST OF ILLUSTRATIONS

The Illustrations in this volume were engraved and printed at the Menpes Press, Watford.

CHAPTER I

THE BEAUTY OF THE RIVER

CLOSE your eyes and conjure up a vision of the river Thames; what is the picture that you see? If you are a prosaic and commercial person, whose business lies by the river side, the vision will be one of wharves and docks, of busy cranes loading and unloading; a row of bonded warehouses rising from the water's edge; lighters filled with tea lying in their shadow, tarpaulined and padlocked; ships of all sizes and shapes, worn by water and weather. And up and down, in and

1

out, among it all you see river police on their launch, inquisitive and determined, watching everything, hearing everything, and turning up when least expected. The glories of the high Tower Bridge, and the smoky gold of the setting sun will not affect you, for your thoughts are fixed on prosaic detail. As for green fields and quiet backwaters, such things do not enter into the vision at all.

Yet for one who sees the Thames thus prosaically, a hundred see it in a gayer aspect. To many a man it is always summer there, for the river knows him not when the chill grey days draw in. He sees gay houseboats in new coats of paint, decorated with scarlet geraniums and other gaudy plants. He associates the river with "a jolly good time" with a carefully chosen house-party, with amateur tea-making and an absence of care. Nowhere else is one so free to "laze" without the rebuke even of one's own occasionally too zealous conscience.

To another the Thames simply means the Boat Race, nothing more and nothing less. Year by year he journeys up to London from his tiny vicarage in the heart of the country for that event. If the high tide necessitates it, he stands shivering on the

brink in the chill whiteness of early morning. He
sits on the edge of a hard wooden cart for an
immense time, and, by way of keeping up his
strength, eats an indigestible penny bun, a thing
that it would never enter his head to do at any other
time. He sees here and there one or the other of
those school-fellows or university chums who have
dropped out of his life for all the rest of the year.
Then, after a moment's shouting, a moment's
tense anxiety or bitter disappointment, according to the position of the boats, the flutter of a
flag, and a thrill of something of the old enthusi-
asm that the unsparing poverty of his life has
slowly ground out of him, he retires to his vicarage
again for another year, elated or depressed according to the result of the race.

To others Henley is the embodiment of all
that is joyous; the one week in the year that is
worth counting. But to others, and these a vast
majority of those who know the river at all, the
Thames means fresh and life-giving air after a
week spent within four walls. It means con-
genial exercise and light, and the refreshment that
beauty gives, even if but half realised. It means a
quiet dream with a favourite pipe in a deep backwater so overhung with trees that it resembles a

green tunnel. The gentle drone of the bees sounds from the banks, there is a flash of blue sheen as a kingfisher darts by; a gentle dip and slight crackling tell of another favoured individual making his way cautiously along to the same sheltered alley; the radiant sunlight falls white upon the water through the leaves and sends shimmering reflections of dancing ripples on the sides of the punt. Such a position is as near Paradise as it is given to mortal to attain.

These are only a few of an inexhaustible variety of aspects of this glorious river, and each reader is welcome to add his own favourite to the list.

For the purposes of this book we are dealing with the Thames between Oxford and London, though as a matter of fact, tradition has it that the Thames proper does not begin until below Oxford, where it is formed by the junction of the Thame and the Isis. Tamese (Thames) means "smooth spreading water." Tam is the same root as occurs in Tamar, etc., and the "es" is the perpetually recurring word for water, *e.g.*, Ouse, ooze, usquebagh. Isis is probably a back formation, from Tamesis. In Drayton's *Polyolbion*, we have the pretty allegory of the wedding of Thame and Isis, from which union is born the sturdy Thames.

PANGBOURNE

Now Fame had through this Isle divulged in every ear
The long expected day of marriage to be near,
That Isis, Cotswold's heir, long woo'd was lastly won,
And instantly should wed with Thame, old Chiltern's son.

In Spenser's *Faerie Queene* the notion is carried one step further, and Thames, the son of Thame and Isis, is to wed with Medway, a far-fetched conceit, for the rivers do not run into each other in any part of their course.

It is strange that a river such as the Thames, which, though by no means great as regards size, has played an important part in the life of the nation, should not have inspired more writers. There is no striking poem on the Thames. The older poets, Denham, Drayton, Spenser, Cowley, Milton, and Pope, all refer to the river more or less frequently, but they have not taken it as a main theme. It is even more neglected by later poets. There are poems to special parts or scenes, such as Gray's well-known "Ode on a Distant Prospect of Eton College"; the river colours one or two of Matthew Arnold's poems; but the great poem, which shall take it as a sole theme, is yet to come. Neither is there a good book on this river, though it is among rivers what London is among the cities of men. Yet the material is abundant, and associations are scattered thickly

along the banks. No fewer than seven royal
palaces have stood by the river. And of these one
is still the principal home of our sovereign. Of
the others, Hampton Court, chiefly reminiscent
of William III., is standing. The neighbouring
palace of Richmond remains but in a fragment.
At London, Westminster, the home of our early and
mediæval kings, has vanished, except for the great
hall and a crypt. Whitehall—the old palace— is
wholly gone, though one part of the new palace
projected by James I. remains. As for the old
palace of Greenwich, so full of memories of the
Tudors, that has been replaced by a later structure.
I hesitate to name Kew in this list, so entirely
unworthy is it of the name of palace, yet, as the
residence of a king it should, perhaps, find a place.

From the annals of these palaces English history
could be completely reconstructed from the time
of Edward the Confessor to the present day.

But it is not in historical memories alone that
the Thames is so rich. Poets, authors, politicians,
and artists have crowded thickly on its banks
from generation to generation. The lower reaches
are haunted by the names of Hogarth, Cowley,
Thomson ; further up we come to the homes of
Walpole, Pope, and Fielding. At Laleham lived

Matthew Arnold. Not far from Magna Charta Island is Horton, where Milton lived. Though his home was not actually on the river, Milton must have often strolled along the banks of the Thames, and many of his poems show the impress of associations gathered from such scenery as is to be found about Ankerwyke and Runneymead :

> Straight mine eye hath caught new pleasures,
> While the landscape round it measures :
> Russet lawns and fallows gray,
> Where the nibbling flocks do stray.
> Meadows trim with daisies pied ;
> Shallow brooks and rivers wide.

From the records of Eton alone many a book might be compiled of the lives of men in the public eye, whose impressions were formed there by the Thames side. Indeed, had the river no other claim to notice than its connection with Eton and Oxford, through which more men who have controlled the destiny of their country and made empire have passed, than through any similar foundations in England, this alone would be cause enough to make it a worthy subject for any book.

Beside palaces and the homes of great men, castles and religious houses once stood thickly along the banks of the river. The notable monasteries of Reading, Dorchester, Chertsey, and

Abingdon, etc., were widely celebrated as seats of learning in their day, and the castles of Reading, Wallingford, and Oxford were no less well known.

It is a curious law in rivers that, as a whole, the windings usually cover double the length of the direct axis, and the Thames is no exception to the rule. It sweeps in and out with a fair amount of regularity, the great bend to the south at Thames Ditton and Weybridge being reversed higher up in the great bend to the north at Bourne End and Hambleden. Naturally the sides of these indentations run north and south instead of in the usual course of east and west. From Wargrave to Henley the current is almost due north, and likewise from Surbiton to Brentford. A more apparent curve, because much smaller in radius, is that at Abingdon; here the course by the stream is about nine miles, in contrast to the two overland. The Great Western Railway is the chief river railway, but as it runs a comparatively straight course between London and Didcot, some places on the great curves are considerably off the main line, and are served by branches. After Reading it keeps very close to the river as far as Moulsford, and is not distant from it the rest

DORCHESTER ABBEY

of the way to Oxford, as it turns almost direct north from Didcot Junction. The Great Western Railway is ably supplemented by the London and South Western Railway, from which the lesser stations on the south of the river near to London can be reached, also the districts of Twickenham, Hampton, etc., included in the chapter called " The Londoners' Zone." Further up, Weybridge, Chertsey, Egham, and Windsor can also be reached by this railway, which cuts a curve and touches the river again at Reading.

There are many zones on the river, and each has its devotees. It is curious to notice how one crowd differs from another crowd on its " people-pestered shores." It is difficult to draw hard and fast lines, but taking the boundaries of the London County Council as the end of London, we can count above it many zones, rich in beauty, divided from each other by stretches of dulness ; for, beautiful as the river is, it must be admitted parts of it are dull, though, like the patches on a fair skin, these serve but to emphasise the character-istics of the remainder. A rather dreary bit succeeds Hammersmith, though this is not without its own attractiveness, and the first real zone that we can touch upon is that from Richmond to

Hampton, which runs Maidenhead hard for first place in popularity; but the Richmond and Hampton river people are largely recruited from the inhabitants, while those at Maidenhead are mostly visitors. Passing over the waterworks and embankments above Hampton, we begin another zone, much less known because less accessible, but in its own way more attractive than that of Richmond. It is pure country, with green fields, willow trees, cows grazing on the banks, many curves and doublings in the channel of the main stream, and ever varying vistas, and this continues to beyond Weybridge. About Chertsey the scenery is flat, but Laleham and Penton Hook are two places that annually delight hundreds of persons.

Between Staines and Windsor there is a fairly attractive stretch, with the park and woods of Ankerwyke on one side, and the meadows on the other. High on the south rises Cooper's Hill, and beyond Albert Bridge we see the smoothly kept turf of the Home Park.

Windsor and Eton, of course, will require a chapter to themselves. In this general description it is sufficient to say that the influence of Eton is apparent all the way to Bray. Then we start a new zone, the most popular one on the river, that from Maidenhead to Bourne End. Of the delights of this beautiful and varied section it is unnecessary here to speak. But the Maidenhead reach is spoilt for fastidious people by its too great popularity. To those who love the river for itself, the endless passing and repassing, the impossibility of finding quiet, undisturbed corners, the noise and merrymaking, even the sight of too many fellow creatures, is a burden. From this the part above Marlow is protected by being less accessible. It is too far to be reached easily from Maidenhead, and those who come by train have an awkward change at a junction; therefore the crowd finds it not. Yet the beauties are no less admirable than those of the adored Maidenhead.

At Hambleden the influence of Henley begins to be felt, and above Henley we enter on another zone. Nowhere else on the river are to be found so many fascinating spots lying in the stream; certainly, no other part offers so many tempting backwaters. This is the zone for those who love the country pure and simple, and who can put up cheerfully with the inconveniences attendant on the procuring of supplies, for the sake of the quiet, marshy meadows.

The reach includes Sonning with its two bridges, its islands, and its rose-garden; but beyond Sonning dulness is apparent once more, and with the neighbourhood of the great and smoky town of Reading, charm withers.   It is not until Mapledurham that the prettiness of the river becomes again apparent, and Mapledurham is rather an oasis, for in the reach beyond it, though the great rounded chalk hills grow opal in the sunlight, and the larks sing heavenwards, the attractiveness cannot be called beauty.   From Pangbourne and Whitchurch to Goring and Streatley, the river lies beneath the chalk heights, which seem to dip underground, reappearing on the other side by Streatley; and the whole of the stretch, with its rich and varied woods, its delightful islands and weirs, its pretty cottages and churches, is full of charm.

Beyond Cleeve Lock, with the single exception of Mongewell, there is again dulness, though for boating pure and simple the reach is very good. Wallingford has a trim prettiness of its own, with its clean-cut stone bridge and its drooping willow. Park-like grounds and pleasant trees succeed, Sinodun Hill looms up ahead, and one may penetrate up the Thame to Dorchester, where the willows nearly meet overhead.   Day's Lock still

DAY'S LOCK

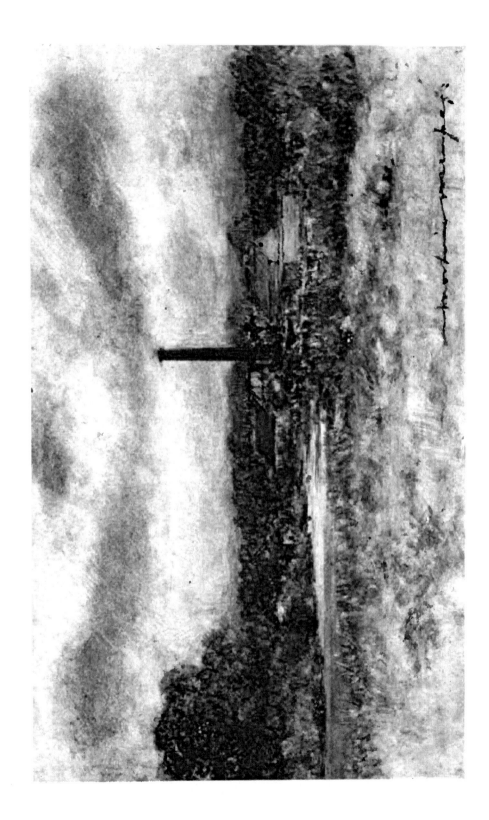

belongs to the clean prettiness of the Wallingford stretch, which, in fact, continues all the way to Culham, notwithstanding that we pass the much admired Clifton Hampden, where the church stands high on the cliff. Culham itself is dull, but with the pretty backwater of Sutton Courtney we begin a new kind of scenery. Abingdon has something of its richness and profusion, and Nuneham Courtney woods, though not rising so abruptly as those at Clieveden, are glorious. After this we begin the famous meadows that continue more or less all the way to Oxford, and have a fascination of their own.

The best way to see the river as a whole, for those who can spare the time, is to go on Salter's steamers, which run daily, Sundays excepted, during the summer. The fare one way is 14s., exclusive of food, and the night spent *en route*. The trip takes two days, the steamer leaving Kingston at 9 in the morning, and reaching Henley at 7.15 in the evening. The reverse way, it leaves Oxford at 9.30, and reaches Henley, which is about half-way, at 7 in the evening.

In this rough sketch it has been shown that there is no lack of choice for those who seek their pleasure on the river, and the opportunity meets with full response. Seen in sunshine on a summer morning, especially if it be the end of the week, the river is brilliant. The dainty coloured muslins and laces, the Japanese parasols, the painted boats, the large shady hats, the sparkle where the oars meet the water, and the white sails of the sailing boats bellying in the wind, are only a few items in a sparkling picture. Fragile, yellow-white butter-flies and the richer coloured red admirals hover about the banks; purple loose-strife, meadow-sweet, and snapdragon grow on the banks with many a tall gaudily coloured weed. Here and there great cedars rise among the lighter foliage, showing black against a turquoise sky; while on the water, where the wind has ruffled it, there is the "many twinkling smile" ascribed by Æschylus to the ocean. But, to those who know the Thames, this smiling aspect is not the only lovable one: they know it also after rain, when the water comes thundering over the weirs in translucent hoops of vivid green, and the boiling foam below dances like whipped cream. To walk along the sedgy banks is to leave a trail of "squish-squash" with every step. All the yellow and brown flat-leaved green things that grow thickly near the edges are barely able to keep their heads above

NEAR THE BRIDGE, SUTTON COURTNEY

the stream, and the long reeds bend with the current like curved swords. Every little tributary gushes gurgling to join in the mad race, and the sounds that tell of water are in our ears like the instruments in an orchestra. There are the rush, the dip, and the tinkle, as well as the deep-throated roar. Watching and listening, we feel a strange sympathy with the new life brought by the increased current; we feel as if it were flooding through our own veins, and as if we, like the squirming, wriggling things that live in the slime below the flood-curtain, were waking up anew after a long torpor.

Even in late autumn, when the slow, white mist rises from the marshy ground, and most of the birds are gone; when the eddies are full of dead leaves floating away from the wood where all their sheltered lives have been spent; when the sparkle and the gaiety and the light-heartedness are gone, and the water looks indigo and dun, with patches of quicksilver floating on it; when the great webs of the spiders that haunt the banks hang like filmy curtains of lace heavy with the moisture of the air, and the sun sinks wanly behind a bank of cloud—even then the river may be loved.

Assuredly, those who go on the river for the day only, and know it but under one aspect—that of lazy heat—lose much. In the evening time, as one steps from the long French window into the scented dusk, soft white moths flap suddenly across the strip of light, and one's feet fall silently on the velvet turf, cool with the freshness that ever is on a river margin. Down by the edge the black water hurries swiftly past with a continuous soothing gurgle. A sleepy bird moves in a startled way in a bush, and all the small things that awake in the night are stirring. One can reach down and touch the onyx water slipping between one's fingers like dream jewels; and far overhead in the rent and torn caverns of the clouds, the stars, bigger and brighter than ever they look in London, sail swiftly and silently from shelter to shelter. The plaintive cry of an owl sounds softly from the meadow across the water, and there is an indescribable sense of motion and poetry, and a thrill of expectation that would be wholly lacking in a landscape ever so beautiful, without the river.

Then there are the grey days, when sudden sheens of silver drop upon the ruffled water as it eddies round a corner, and in a moment the surface is peopled with dancing fairies, spangled and brilliant, flitting in and out in bewildering movement. Or the same cold, silver light catches the side of a ploughed field, a moment before brown, but now shot with green as all the long delicate blades are revealed. These, and a thousand other delights, cannot be known to the visitor of a day only. Under all its aspects, in all its vagaries, the river may be loved ; and in the swift gliding motion there is an irresistible fascination. It gives meaning to idleness, and fills up vacancy. By the banks of the river one never can be dull.

The river is one of the greatest of our national possessions. Other rivers there are in England where one may boat on a small part, where here and there are beauty spots ; but the Thames alone gives miles of bewildering choice, and can take hundreds and hundreds at once upon its flood. Now embanked and weired and locked, its waters are ideal for boating, and its fishing, with little exception, is free to all.

Shooting on the banks of the Thames is forbidden, and the birds have quickly learned to know their sanctuary. Lie still for a while in the lee of an osier-covered ait, or beneath the shelter of an overhanging willow, and that cheeky little reed-

bunting will hop about so near, that, were you
endowed by nature with the quickness of movement granted to a cat, you could seize it in
one hand.   White-throats, robins, thrushes, black-
birds, all haunt the stream, and reed warblers
and sedge warblers have their haunts by the
banks.   The kingfisher is rapidly increasing, and
makes his home quite close to the locks and weirs ;
the russet brown of his breast, as he sits motionless
on a twig waiting his time for a dart, may now
be seen by a noiseless and sharp-eyed watcher.
The soft coo of the wood pigeons sounds from
tall trees, and the cawing of the rooks, softened by
distance into a melodious conversation, is wafted
from many a rookery.   The chatter of an impudent
magpie may worry you, or the hoarse squawk
of a jay break your rest, but they are only the
discords that the great musician, Nature, knows
how to introduce into her river symphony.

Hotels on the river have, in the last few years,
awakened to the cry of the middle classes for air
and light, and yet more air.   Some of the hotels
are pretty with verandahs and creeper covered
walls, but others are old-fashioned—with low
rooms.   Yet every proprietor who can by hook or
crook manage it, now runs a lawn of exquisite

STREATLEY INN

turf down to the water's edge, decorates it with flowers far more vivid than can be seen elsewhere, and knocks up a bungalow-like building, terribly desolate in the winter when the green mould creeps insidiously over the wooden posts, and the sail-cloth rots in the damp; but airy and commodious in the summer, when relays of fifty people or more may be seated at a time, and yet there is no satiating smell of cooked food. The boat owners have also seen fit to accommodate their convenience to the demand, and at any large builder's landing-stage, boats may now be hired to be left almost anywhere on the river, to be fetched back by the owner.

Pessimists say that the river is losing its charm, that the advent of motor cars, stirring in people a hitherto dormant love of speed, makes the slow progress of punting a weariness instead of a relaxation. But this is not greatly to be feared. The charm of a motor is one thing, the charm of the river another; and we cannot spare either. Crowds may slightly diminish, but this is no loss, rather a gain to the real river lover.

Thames gardens are peculiar. By the nature of the case they must be far more public than ordinary gardens, for the owner's reason for

3

buying the house was that he wanted to sit on his own green turf and see the river flow endlessly past. Therefore, though he may hedge around the three land sides with high walls and impenetrable thorns, he leaves the fourth side open so that all the world may look. No one has yet been clever enough to invent a screen that shall be transparent on one side and opaque on the other, and until they do, the owners of these beautiful river lawns must sit in the full light that beats upon the river banks, and allow every passing stranger who has raked up a shilling to hire a boat, to enjoy the beauties of a garden he has not paid for. Thames lawns are celebrated, and rightly so. Not even the turf of college quads, grown for hundreds of years, can beat their turf. Thick, smooth, closely woven they are, and above all, of a pure rich green that is a delight to see, and, by way of enhancing this marvellous green, the colour which is most often to be seen with it is its complementary colour, red. Whether the effect is obtained merely by contrast I do not know, but certainly it seems as if nowhere else could be found geraniums of so rich a vermilion, roses of so glorious a crimson. In many of these river gardens, too, especially where a little stream trickles down, a light trellis arch is thrown up and covered with Rambler roses, old rose in colour, and only second to the vermilion as a complement to the green lawn.

Two of these gloriously green lawns I have particularly in mind, one at Shepperton, and one near Thames Ditton, but where they are to be seen so frequently it is invidious to particularise.

These are the private gardens of a grand sort, and no whit less beautiful, though without the same expanse of lawn, are the gardens of the lock-keepers, in which the owners take a particular pride.

> Soon will the musk carnations break and swell,
> Soon shall we have gold-dusted snapdragon,
> Sweet-william with his homely cottage smell,
> And stocks in fragrant blow ;
> Roses, that down the alleys shine afar,
> And open, jasmine-muffled lattices.
> —*M. Arnold.*

But in taking count of Thames's decorations we are not confined to gardens. Among the flowers growing wild on the river banks we have no lack of choice. It is a pretty conceit of Drayton's, to make his bridal pair, Thame and Isis, travel to meet one another along paths flower-decked by willing nymphs. Old Thame, as the man, was to have only wild flowers, not those "to gardens that belong":

The primrose placing first because that in the spring
It is the first appears, then only flourishing,
The azured harebell next, with them they neatly mix'd,
T'allay whose luscious smell, they woodbind plac'd betwixt.
Amongst those things of scent, there prick they in the lily;
And near to that again her sister daffodilly.
To sort these flowers of show with th' other that were sweet
The cowslip then they couch, and th' oxlip, for her meet,
The columbine amongst they sparingly do set,
The yellow king-cup wrought in many a curious fret,
And now and then among, of eglantine a spray,
By which again a course of lady smocks they lay
The crow flower, and thereby the clover-flower they stick.
The daisie over all those sundry sweets so thick;

     *   *   *   *

The crimson darnel flowers, the blue-bottle and gold
Which, though esteemed but weeds, yet for their dainty hues
And for their scent not ill, they for this purpose choose.

The "luscious smell" cannot refer to the harebell, which has a very faint perfume; besides, it is difficult to think of the harebell in this connection, for it is a full summer flower, while all the rest belong to spring: Drayton must, therefore, mean the wild hyacinth, which is still often called the bluebell by people in England, though in Scotland this name is correctly reserved for the harebell. The "luscious smell" exactly describes the rich, rather cloying scent of the hyacinth. There has been some discussion as to what is meant by the eglantine, which the old poets are so fond of mentioning. In Milton it means the honeysuckle, but in the others probably the sweetbriar; while woodbine is either the twining clematis, the "traveller's joy"—rather a misnomer, by-the-way, as it is an insignificant and disappointing flower—or the honeysuckle.

Isis was gay with garden flowers:

. . . The brave carnation then,
With th' other of his kind, the speckled and the pale,
Then th' odoriferous pink, that sends forth such a gale
Of sweetness, yet in scents as various as in sorts.
The purple violet then, the pansy there supports
The marygold above t' adorn the arched bar;
The double daisie, thrift, the button bachelor,
Sweet-william, sops-in-wine, the campion, and to these
Some lavender they put with rosemary and bays.

To make a catalogue of the flowers which may be found on the Thames banks at the present day would be out of place here, yet there are one or two plants so frequently seen that they may be mentioned. Among these are the purple loose-strife, with its tapering, richly coloured spikes, standing sometimes as high as four feet, and occasionally mistaken for a foxglove; the pink-flowered willow-herb; the wild mustard or cherlock, with its sulphur yellow blossoms, and creeping-jenny. The bog-bean, or buck-bean, with white lace-like flowers may be seen occasionally in stagnant swamps. The water-violet, which, however, is not in the least like a violet, is also to be found in the tributary ditches, as well as the tall yellow iris; the flowering rush and the bur-reeds often form details in a river picture. In the lock gardens herbaceous borders, full of phlox, sweet-william, stocks, valerian, big white lilies, and, later, red hot pokers, sunflowers, and holly-hocks, are ordinary sights. In the meadows near Oxford fritillaries, otherwise called snakes'-heads, are seen abundantly in spring, but these and other flowers shall be mentioned more particularly in connection with the places where they grow.

It remains but to end with the aspiration of Denham:

> O could I flow like thee, and make thy stream
> My great example as it is my theme !
> Though deep, yet clear; though gentle, yet not dull;
> Strong, without rage; without o'erflowing full.

CHAPTER II

THE OXFORD MEADOWS

This account of the river may well begin at Folly Bridge, seeing it is folly in any case to attempt to cut off a section of a river, and, as before explained, our course from Oxford to London is peculiarly arbitrary, for the Thames proper does not begin till below Dorchester, and at Oxford the river is the Isis. Having thus disarmed criticism, without further explanation or apology, we stand upon Folly Bridge, which

25

is a little way above the end of the course for both Torpids and Eights.

To the left are the college barges, resplendent in many colours, with their slender flagstaffs rising against a background of the shady trees that border Christchurch meadows. The reach of water beside them is alive with boats, and the oars rise and dip with the regularity of the legs of a monster centipede. The barges should be seen in Eights week, when they are in their glory, occupied by the mothers, sisters, and aunts of the undergraduates, dressed in costumes that in mass look like brilliant flower-beds.

To see the bridge properly, however, it is necessary to go down to the tow-path and look back at it, when its quaint, foreign appearance can be better estimated. It stands across an island on which is the renowned Salter's boat-house, and its solidity and the tall houses near it, which throw black shadows in the yellow sunlight, make it look not unlike a corner in Venice.

Following the river down, we see on the Oxford side the narrow mouth of the meandering Cherwell under a white arched bridge. The most delightful place for "lazing" in a boat is the Cherwell, shady and not too wide; deliciously cool in the height of the summer, so rich is the foliage of the over-arching trees. Lower down is the New Cut, destined to relieve the Cherwell of its superfluous water in flood time and so prevent the flooding of the Christchurch meadows. Opposite the mouth of the New Cut is the University Boat-house, and further down, where a branch of the river runs off to the right, are the bathing places. This branch is crossed by a bridge, and it makes the next strip of land an island. The place is known as the Long Bridges. The river narrows at the point, and the narrowed part is called The Gut; just below a tributary from the Cherwell, known as the Freshman's river, dribbles into the Thames. It is at The Gut that the most exciting scenes in the races generally happen. As everyone knows, Torpids are in the fourth and fifth weeks after the beginning of the Lent term, and as they are not of so much importance as the Eights, and as the weather does not lend itself to open-air festivities, they are generally watched only by a shivering handful of spectators who have a more or less personal interest in them. The Eights, which take place in the middle of the summer term, are the event of the year to Oxford, and intensely exciting they may be. The lowest boat starts from the lasher above Iffley, and the course ends at Salter's Barge. But the crux of the whole matter often lies in The Gut, and much depends on the ability of the cox to steer a clean course, as to whether his boat is bumped or bumps. As the boats in cutting the curve below this crucial point come diagonally at it, disaster here often overtakes a crew which has before been doing well. The aforesaid narrow channel from the Cherwell is navigable only in a canoe and by good luck; but the tale is told that one cox, in his first year, being excited beyond reason, mistook it for the main channel, and, steering right ahead, landed his crew high and dry on the shoals. Hence the name, the Freshman's river.

Here are two pictures, taken from life, which express the difference between the two occasions:

The Eights: Brilliant blue sky above, glinting blue water beneath. Down across Christchurch meadow troops a butterfly crowd, flaunting brilliant parasols and chattering gaily to the "flannelled fools" who form the escort. Despite the laughter it is a solemn occasion, for the college boat that is head of the river may be going to be bumped this afternoon, and, if so, the bump will surely take place in front of the barges. The only question is, before which barge will it happen? When the exciting moment draws near, chatter ceases, a tense stillness holds the crowd in thrall; the relentless pursuers creep on steadily, narrowing the gap between themselves and the first boat, and finally

bump it exactly opposite its own barge ! A moment's pause. The completeness of the triumph is too impressive to be grasped at once; then—pandemonium! Pistol-shots, rattles, hoots, yells, shrieks of joy, wildly waving parasols, and groans.

The Torpids : A raw cold February day ; a leaden sky heavy with snow ; dimly seen figures scudding over the frozen meadows of Iffley ; the river itself is almost frost-bound, and the men waiting in the boats for the starting gun look blue and pinched. They must find these last ten seconds hard to endure. Nine, eight, seven, six—ugh ! will it never go? At last ! And, as the signal sounds, the oars strike the water with a splash, and the boats shoot off and begin the long tussle against a head wind and that strong stream which always makes the Torpids a harder matter than the Eights rowed in summer water. It is too late to follow them, so heigh-ho for the King's Arms Hotel at Sandford, and a cup of the good hot tea that the landlady knows so well how to make !

The channel running past the bathing places is equally unsuited for navigation, and is moreover guarded by two mills, but it may be negotiated with the aforesaid element of good luck. Hinksey Stream flows into this backwater, and there are several places, after shoals have been avoided or surmounted, where it is extremely pleasant to while away an idle hour. By means of the Long Bridges and the lock at Iffley it is possible to get across the river from side to side diagonally. Passing on down stream we soon come to Iffley. In the meantime we can see many of the pinnacles

4

and spires and domes for which Oxford is famous,
and marvellous is the way in which they appear to
swing round as we change our position. The part
of new Oxford which lines the Iffley road behind
the meadows is not attractive, but when we come
in sight of Iffley itself we may well exclaim that
it would be hard to find a sweeter spot. There are
stone walls, thatched cottages and farmyards, hay
and orchards, elms, alders, and silver-stemmed
birches; in consequence a quiet, rural atmosphere
broods over all. The cows feed down to the edge of
the river, and swallows dart about overhead, while
perhaps a man paddling a canoe shoots up and away
again, his white flannels and the strength and grace
of his movement irresistibly recalling a swan. The
mill, half stone, half wooden cased, is very ancient;
the massive foundations have become like rock
from their long immersion in the running water.
There is a great quiet pool behind the lock island,
and here and there a glimpse may be caught of the
square tower of the famous church, which is not
far off, but is well hidden by trees.

Iffley Church takes rank with Stewkley as the
most beautiful example of a Norman church
remaining to us out of London. It is, like so
many Norman churches, very small and very solid.

And it must yield to Stewkley in the fact that its architecture is not pure. Yet its massive central tower and its fine windows place it very high indeed. Its date is not certainly known, but is supposed to be between 1160 and 1170. "The interior seems at first sight curious. There are, in fact, two chancels, one behind the other. The further one is early English work, and is much lighter in style than the rest of the building, and the east end is disappointing. This may have been added to lengthen the church. In the bay next to it, where the choir now sit, there are fourteenth century windows inserted under Norman arches, showing that the walls were of the earlier date. These windows were added by John de la Pole, Duke of Suffolk, in the latter half of the sixteenth century. There is a groined roof, and the piers are beautifully decorated. The arches supporting the tower are richly moulded, almost incongruously so in regard to the massive type of the masonry, which points to early Norman. The Perpendicular windows inserted in the north and south walls are good. It is only at the extreme west end that the Norman windows remain untouched. The font is of black marble, and is very curious. The triple west-end window, a splendid specimen, is best seen from the churchyard. Its moulding is very rich, and this alone would be sufficient to make Iffley rank high among ancient churches. Below it is a circular window inserted about 1858 on the supposed plan of a former one of which traces were found. The impossibility of approaching the style of the old work in modern times was never more strikingly shown. Below is a fine doorway with beak-head and billet moulding, worthy to be classed with the triple window. A very ancient yew stands on the south side of the church, and near it is the slender shaft of an old cross. The rectory house, dating from Tudor times, is a fine addition to the picturesque group."—*Guide to the Thames*.

Between Iffley and Sandford the famous Oxford meadows are seen at their best. In the summer they are gemmed with countless flowers, so that they rival the celebrated Swiss pastures. Prominent among these is the fritillary:

> I know what white, what purple fritillaries
> The grassy harvest of the river-fields,
> Above by Ensham, down by Sandford yields,
> And what sedged brooks are Thames's tributaries.
>
> —*M. Arnold.*

Mr. G. Claridge Druce, the well-known botanist, who has made a special study of the Thames

Valley and Oxfordshire, says:—" The Thames from Oxford to Sandford flows through meadows rich with fritillaries, its banks are bordered with the sweet-scented Acorus, and its waters are inhabited by Potamogeton prœlongus, flabellatus, and compressus, Zannichellia macrostemon, Œnanthe fluviatilis, &c., and near Sandford appears, for the first time in the river's course, the lovely Leucojum æstivum." This is the flower better known as the summer snowflake, which we shall meet again. The above are only a tithe of the flowers which Mr. Druce mentions. Among others which may be recognised are the yellow iris, the cuckoo flower, the water villarsia, the purple orchis, and the willow weed. In the spring the marsh mallow is the first to appear with a vivid glory as of sunshine. The banks are flat and low, and, except for the flowers, uninteresting ; nevertheless this is a useful part of the river, especially for sailing. Some college fours are rowed here. Passing under the railway line we see the pink-washed walls of the Swan Hotel, which stands on Kennington Island, connected with the mainland by a bridge ; and then we come to Sandford itself, with charms almost as great as, though entirely different from, those of Iffley.

The approach is disappointing. The tall mill chimney and the new brick houses are bare and ugly. The mill is a paper mill, and supplies the Clarendon Press. It stands close to the old-fashioned and pretty hotel, so completely ivy-covered that even one of the tall chimneys is quite overgrown. When close to the lock the mill is not noticeable and has the advantage of affording some shelter. As at Iffley, one can get right across from bank to bank by means of bridges, a most charming method that might well be adopted in other parts of the river. Indeed, near Oxford one great delight is the freedom from interference. Everyone is allowed full liberty; you may ride your bicycle along the tow-path, take it across locks, or even walk it by the side of the meadows, without any rebuke. Having put up a notice that they are not responsible for the condition of the tow-path and that people use it at their own risk, the Conservancy leave the matter alone. The islands at Sandford are rather complicated, and there are a couple of weirs, beneath which the water frills out over mossy stones into deep, shady pools. The fishing here is as good as any on the river. The Radley College boat-house and bathing place are near the lower pool, the

RADLEY COLLEGE BOAT-HOUSE

college itself being rather more than a mile away. In spring these pools, with their broken banks of brown earth and their masses of scented white hawthorn, are most beautiful. The shy white violets hide in the grass near the weirs, and are found by only a few who know where to seek them.

In the Oxford zone we must include the woods at Nuneham Courtney, which, by the courtesy of the owner (Aubrey Harcourt), are open to undergraduates all Commemoration week and twice a week in the summer term; while the general public, after writing in advance, are allowed to picnic at the lock cottages two days a week from May to September. The Nuneham woods are on a ridge of greensand, and though they are not so high or at such a striking angle as those of Clieveden, they certainly have quite as great a charm. Anyone is allowed to walk through the park if it be approached from the road, but bicycles are not permitted. The lock cottages, which are a popular resort in the summer, stand beside a pretty wooden bridge which connects the islands with the mainland. Masses of wild roses and flowering clematis add their delicate touch to the beauty of the overhanging trees. Close by the water is the Carfax monument, a conduit or fountain erected by Otho Nicholson, who set it up at the place still called Carfax in Oxford, whence it was removed to its present position in 1787. The woods contain nothing very striking in the way of trees, though all the commoner sorts, the beeches, oaks, horse-chestnuts, and so on, are well represented. There are about 400 acres of wood, which surround the park, where the oaks show well, standing apart from each other.

CHAPTER III

THE OLD TOWN OF ABINGDON

As a headquarters for boating, for those who want to dawdle and explore odd corners and have no desire to rush through as many locks as possible in a day, Abingdon makes a good centre. It is within easy reach of the part lying below the woods at Nuneham, and in the other direction is the Sutton Courtney backwater, which, Wargrave notwithstanding, is not to be beaten on the Thames. Further down again is Clifton Hampden, which attracts many people, and the river at Abingdon

itself is by no means to be despised. The bridge,
called Burford Bridge, is a real delight. It is old
and irregular, with straggling arches, some rounded,
some pointed ; and all, even the highest, comparatively low down over the water, framing cool, dark
shadows within the embrace of the mighty piers.
The bridge cannot be seen in the glance of an eye.
It is very long, and rests partly on an island.
Standing on this, the Nag's Head Inn projects
from one side of the bridge, and from it stretches
out a small garden with several orchard trees.
The red tiles and creamy tint of the hotel walls
show well in contrast with the grey stone of the
bridge, and when the hotel is seen from the river
above the bridge, with the tall spire of St. Helen's
Church rising behind it, it is worth noticing.

There are bits of old wall lining the bank on the
town side, and ivy grows freely over them. Many
of the houses stand back from the water; a part
of the ruined abbey and the long range of the
abbot's residence can be seen between masses of
blossom. The great exterior chimney of the abbey
buildings should particularly be noticed. The
blossom at Abingdon is a great feature, and one
not to be found everywhere. Horse-chestnuts and
holm oaks dip their boughs in the water, and from

ABINGDON

the branches arises a perfect chorus of birds. Abingdon has its chimneys, of course, as well as hideous
buildings suited to modern requirements of business,
but in the general view these things are lost sight of.

Burford is a corruption of Borough-ford, and
before the building of the bridge in the fifteenth
century, the ferry at Culham was the main means
of communication with the other side of the river.

The range of Nuneham, below which runs the
backwater called the Old River, can be seen to the
south-east. If this ever was the main stream it
must have been very long ago, for the memory of
it is not recorded in any document now extant.
The Old River is crossed by another bridge, and
the two are linked by a straight road, made by
Geoffrey Barbour at the same time as the building
of the bridges. There is a picture of Barbour
in the almshouses, and this shows the bridge being
built in the background ; while an illuminated copy
of verses tells us :

> King Herry the Fyft, in his fourthe yere,
> He hath i-founde for his folke a brige in Berkschire,
> For cartis with cariage may go and come clere,
> That many wynters afore were mareed in the myre.
> Culham hithe [*wharf or landing*] hath caused many a curse,
> I-blessed be our helpers we have a better waye,
> Without any peny for cart and for horse.

Below Burford Bridge, the great bur-reeds grow near the islands. There is one delightful old house, formerly a malt house, with all sorts of odd angles and corners. It encloses a small terraced court, from which steps lead down to the water. It stands on the site of St. Helen's nunnery, founded about 690. Further on are some of the newer almshouses—a blot on the scene; and then a glimpse may be had of the wooden cloister of the old almshouses, which, in their way, are as pretty as those at Bray.

Christ's Hospital, as the almshouses are called, was founded in the reign of Edward VI. out of lands belonging to a dissolved Guild of the Holy Cross. The central hall dates, however, from 1400. It has a stone mullioned window and panelled walls; in the ceiling is a dome or cupola. Once a week eighty loaves of bread are here distributed among the poor people of the town, and when the loaves, with their crisp, flaky, yellow crust, stand in piles on the polished oak table, and the poor old people gather for their share, there is an old-world touch in the picture such as one does not often see nowadays. The cloister or arcade of dark wood outside is decorated with texts and proverbs on its inner wall. The newer almshouses, built in 1797,

THE MILL AT ABINGDON

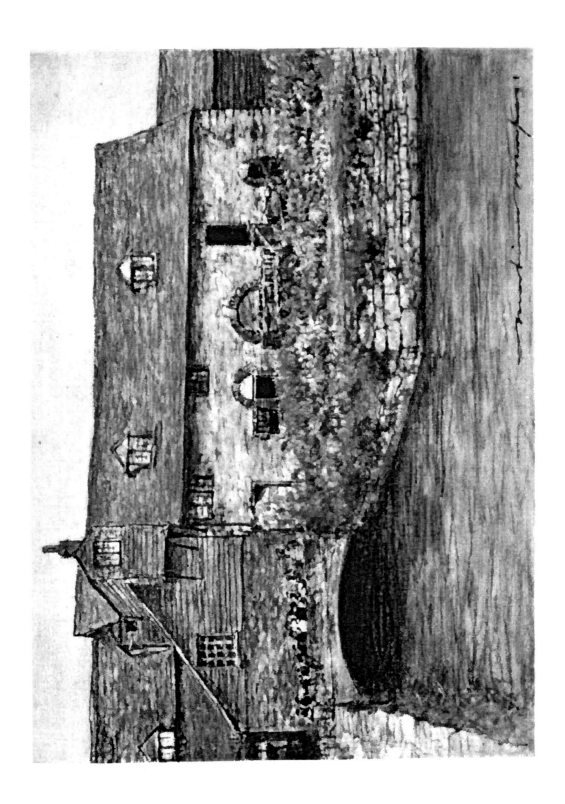

lack all the homeliness and interest of the older ones. The church of St. Helen's, which has a very tall spire, is close to the almshouses and the river, and is well worthy of its position. It has been much restored, but is mainly of sixteenth century work.

Of course there was an abbey at Abingdon, though whether the name of the town arose from that fact or from a proper name Aben or Æbba is doubtful. The earliest name of the town was the unpronounceable one of Seovechesham, and it was then a royal residence. The abbey was founded by Cissa about 675. It was destroyed by the Danes and reconstructed long before most places on the river had begun to have any history at all. The abbey rose to great importance and wealth. It held manors innumerable, and its abbot was a person to reckon with. Even at the date of Domesday Book the abbey held no less than thirty manors. But its power did not save it, and it suffered the common fate at the Dissolution. A gateway of about the fourteenth century and some ruins, which show where the dwellings of the monks stood, are all that remain, beside the guest-chamber —a large, barn-like building—and the almoner's residence. The latter has a magnificent fireplace and chimney. The ceiling of the room below is groined, and looks like that of a crypt, but this is said to have been the kitchen. The chief feature of interest is the huge chimney, which is like a room, and has little windows on each side; its size is best appreciated from the exterior view. The church has quite disappeared, for the little ancient church near the gateway was not the abbey church, but is supposed to have been at first a chapel of ease. In this there is some Norman work, including the west doorway, and it is probably of quite as ancient lineage as anything now remaining of the abbey.

Henry I. was sent by his father, as a lad of twelve, to be educated at Abingdon Abbey, and the learning by which he gained the name of Beauclerc shows that there must have been some able men here. The town hall in the market place at Abingdon is really a fine bit of work. It has been attributed to Inigo Jones, and stands over an open arcade, according to the style of town halls of the seventeenth century. The lock is a good way above Abingdon, and from it the millstream, as usual a pleasant backwater, flows right back to the town, enclosing a large island.

The lock at Culham is one of the least interest-

SUTTON COURTNEY BACKWATER

ing on the river, and of the hundreds who pass
through it only a few know that they are close to
the very prettiest backwater on the Thames,
namely Sutton Pool. There is one backwater at
Sutton Courtney which can be reached from above
Culham Lock. This leads to the mill, now disused,
and runs along the top of the numerous weirs that
pour into Sutton Pool itself. It is pretty also, and
it is pleasant to see the meadows where the cows
stand knee-deep in flowering plants, and the little
square tower of the church peeping through the
trees. This backwater is the best for landing to
go to the village. Along the top of the weirs runs
a path—a public right-of-way—which leads across
the fields to Culham Lock, and anyone may land
here and look down upon the pool; but to get
right into it the lock must be passed, and some
way further, after going under the bridge, we can
turn the corner of a large island and retrace our
way upstream until we come into the great pool,
with its miniature bays and tumbling water. The
weirs are high, and the streams come down with
force, making a restless heave and swell when the
river is full. The little tongues of land that divide
one bay from another are shaded by willows, and
the lush green grass grows here and there around

tiny beaches of white sand. In spring, masses of hawthorn, "all frosted" with flowers, bend down from above, and the wild hyacinths break up between the blades of grass. Tall reeds form tiny islets, and perhaps a little moorhen flaps out. It is in secluded places like this that the dainty nest of the reed-warbler may be seen, swinging so lightly upon its supports that it is extraordinary to think that so large a bird as the cuckoo should dare to deposit its egg there. Yet reed-warblers and sedge-warblers are both among the cuckoo's victims. Unfortunately, in this little paradise landing is everywhere strictly forbidden, but no one can forbid enjoyment of the beauties which appeal to sight.

The village of Sutton Courtney is certainly worth visiting. The village green, with its tall chestnuts, limes, and elms, is the very picture of what a green should be. The church is particularly interesting, for it is that rarity an unrestored building, with the old red-tiled floor and the rudeness of the original—so often smoothed away behind stencilling and paint—still left untouched. There is a shelf of chained books, a fine carved screen, and an altar-tomb of some interest. The manor house, which is not far off, is in a medley of styles,

CLIFTON HAMPDEN FROM THE BRIDGE

ranging from Norman to Jacobean. Malefactors are said to have been hanged from the stout oak beam which is still in good preservation. One wing is of perfect Jacobean work, with an overhanging storey decorated with carved pendants. A fine old building, half-way up the village, is called the Hall of Justice; this, however, may have a meaning less obvious than supposed at first sight, as the family of Justice held the manor for some generations.

In it there is a fine old Norman doorway. The owner has furnished the interior with tapestry hangings, etc., somewhat in accordance with what it may have looked like originally when in use. It certainly gives one an idea of the old Saxon or Norman style of dwelling before even the upper chamber or *solar* came into fashion.

The river at Clifton Hampden is not a couple of miles from the river at Nuneham Courtney, so great is the loop by Abingdon. It may be noted that the name Courtney, though spelt differently, is derived from the ownership of the Courtenays, Earls of Exeter, in both the instances above. Clifton Hampden is a great favourite with artists, for the church, with its little, pointed spire, stands on a cliff which has in parts broken away, showing the rich yellow ochre of the soil. This makes up well in a "composition." The river sweeps round beneath it in a sort of little bay, and when white ducks dabble in the water and blue-pinafored children play beneath the yellow-ochre cliff, there is much to be said for it. The houses, too, are not without points. They are mostly thatched, and have their share of plants and creepers. The bridge is of red brick, and, with a little toning by weather, will make a capital accessory. But to my mind Clifton Hampden lacks that indefinable quality of charm found in such abundance elsewhere.

CLIFTON HAMPDEN

CHAPTER IV

SINODUN HILL AND DORCHESTER

THE island near Day's Lock, lying beneath the Wittenham Woods and Sinodun Hill, is particularly well kept and neat, and, in summer, bright with flowers. Standing on the end of the lock-keeper's island you can look straight up the weir, below which the river drifts away on each side of the island.

On the right bank, raised slightly above the river, is the church of Little Wittenham, with a long, narrow bastion turret adhering to its tower. Inside there is a handsome monument, one of

47

those legacies from the ages that prove long descent. A warm belt of Scotch firs grows near.

Wittenham Woods lie under the shelter of the hill and close to the life-giving water. The trees grow well and form a home for countless birds of all kinds. "The hobby breeds there yearly. The wild pheasant, crow, sparrowhawk, kestrel, magpie, jay, ring-dove, brown owl, water-hen (on the river-bounded side); in summer the cuckoo and turtle-dove are all found there, and, with the exception of the pigeons and kestrels, which seek their food at a distance during the day, they seldom leave the shelter of its trees."—*C. J. Cornish.*

Sinodun Hill, and its companion, Harp Hill, which is as like it as one twin to another, are sometimes called Wittenham Clumps. They are remarkable and conspicuous objects, rising abruptly and evenly from a very flat district, and they can be seen from many miles around, and, what is more curious, can be recognised. The smooth, rounded cone is so symmetrical that, whichever way you look at it, it seems the same, not changing its shape in the bewildering way of most hills; and the clump of trees placed so exactly on its crown is an unfailing river-mark. Sinodun is about 250 feet in height, and on it is

COTTAGES, DORCHESTER

a British earthwork, a triple line of entrenchment, with vallum and foss all round. The circumference of this on the outside is about a mile. Harp Hill has on it a tumulus called Brightwell Barrow. Then down below, close to Dorchester, is a double line of earthworks, much mutilated, but quite noticeable. No one knows the origin of these defences, which date far back into unhistorical days. Those on Sinodun are called British, while the others are supposed to be Roman. Roman camps were nearly always square, while British followed the windings of the hill.

Dorchester, with its cornfields and trees, its vegetable gardens, and its old houses bowed this way and that, is a very unsophisticated little place. The deep quiet of its village street, where the cottages glow all hues in the sunlight, from deep red ochre to egg-colour, brooded over by the long-backed abbey church, is a rest-cure in itself. The great yew trees, the pretty lych-gate, the old wooden porch, are all just what one would expect to find. Dorchester is not on the Thames, yet belongs to it certainly, for the Thame, which combines with the Isis to form the Thames, flows past it. As its name proclaims, Dorchester was once a Roman camp. Numerous Roman coins have been found in the neighbourhood, and a Roman altar. It was also the seat of one of the first and largest bishoprics in England.

In 634 a monk of the order of St. Benedict, named Birinus, crossed to Britain to follow in the steps of St. Augustine and work as a missionary among the men of Wessex. He landed safely, and came to this part of the country, then in Wessex, which at that time stretched north of the Thames, though afterwards, when Mercia's power became great under King Offa, Dorchester fell within that kingdom. Birinus preached with so much effect that the King conferred upon him the office of bishop and gave him Dorchester for his residence. He died in 650 and was buried in his own church, though it is said his body was afterwards moved to Winchester.

The early bishopric was vast. It included what in our own day are the Sees of Bath and Wells, Exeter, Hereford, Lichfield, Lincoln, Salisbury, Worcester, and Winchester. There must have been a church in some degree adequate to the importance of such a charge, but it was probably of wood; in any case, nothing remains of it, though certain indications seem to show that it stood on the same site as the present one.

WHITE HART HOTEL, DORCHESTER

Dorchester was an important city, but its glory did not long remain, and the bishopric was ultimately split up into many Sees. In 1085 the seat of the See of Mercia was transferred to Lincoln. The abbey was founded here in 1140 for Augustinian monks, and it is the monks' church which still in great part exists. The long nave, with its red roof, is seen easily from the river, but the tower appears rather inadequate in height. On approaching, however, it is found to be of massive work. The interior of the church is wide and high, and gives that impression of bareness which is consistent with Norman work. In the east window is a great pier or transom which is supposed to have been originally intended as the support for a groined roof. The north chancel window is the famous Jesse window, with carved tracery, carrying figures all the way up the numerous branches. The lowest is that of Jesse, from whom spring all the subsequent ones. Very few figures are missing, considering the age of the window, and the carving is remarkably interesting. It is supposed that the figures of the Virgin and Child were at one time above that of the patriarch, but were removed at the Reformation. The rich green glass in the sedilia on the other side of the chancel should be noted. It is unusual to see sedilia pierced. Two of the nave arches are plain Norman work. A rood door remains, and there are one or two handsome altar tombs; also a leaden font, well moulded, and, on the east wall of the south aisle, there are some remains of frescoes. Close to the porch outside is a graceful shaft with a "restored" head.

The Thame we have already spoken of. Its arching trees and corners, and deep shady alleys, make it a delightful place for an idler. It runs close by the abbey church.

In the river near Dorchester grow the sweet sedge and the amphibious yellow cress, and on the banks may be found the blue pimpernel.

DORCHESTER BACKWATER

CHAPTER V

CASTLE AND STRONGHOLD

WALLINGFORD boasts of having the oldest corporation in England, preceding that of London by a hundred years, and its record certainly reaches very far back. In 1006 it was destroyed by the Danes. William the Conqueror rested here on his way to London after the battle of Hastings. The town was then held by Wigod, a noble Saxon, who lived in his great fortress-castle. His son-in-law was Robert D'Oyley, who built the castle at Oxford, and rebuilt and

53

greatly strengthened that at Wallingford. From the part of the river above the bridge a tree-grown mound can be seen, and, further back, a comparatively modern house. On the mound once stood the strong castle, and the modern house is its present - day representative. The grounds are famous for their trees, and particularly for their evergreens, which grow thickly on the slopes of what was once the inner castle moat, for there were no less than three. No wonder Queen Maud felt that in reaching Wallingford in safety after her terrible escape over the frozen meadows of Oxford, she once more held the lead in the game she and Stephen played for the crown. Stephen, however, was not daunted. He settled down at Crowmarsh across the river, and made strenuous attempts to take the fortress. After a long time, when the garrison were beginning to despair, the Queen's son Henry came to the rescue with a force sufficient to afford relief. It was at Wallingford the treaty was made which eventually secured Henry's succession. The castle was given to Piers Gaveston by Edward II., but after the fall of Gaveston it reverted to the Crown. Joan, the Fair Maid of Kent, wife of the Black Prince, died here in 1385, and later, in the Civil Wars between King and

WALLINGFORD

Parliament, Wallingford held stoutly to the Stuarts. The town was the last place in Berkshire which remained to the King, and it was taken in July, 1646, after a siege of sixty-five days. Cromwell, therefore, cherished a grudge against it, and when he came into power he ordered the castle to be destroyed, an order which was unfortunately carried out. Not far away in the same grounds is a fragment of a ruined and ivy-grown tower. This is part of an ancient college of St. Nicholas founded by Edmund, second Earl of Cornwall, who died in 1300.

In some ways Wallingford reminds one of Abingdon. They are both homely, pleasant, brick-built market-towns, rather sleepy, but self-respecting. There are several islands beside the bridge; but Wallingford has not made the most of its islands. They are bare, and disfigured by boat-building works. The bridge is fair, and, seen from below, where a weeping willow falls softly over one bank, the view is pretty. A conspicuous feature is the steeple of the church near, looking as if it had been joined on to the body without any thought of continuity of style. There are three churches in Wallingford, which once owned fourteen! There is rather a good seventeenth century Town Hall in the market-place and a Corn Exchange. Friday is the market-day. Both above and below the town the river is pleasant, though without original features ; there are well-kept parks and fine-grown trees to be seen frequently. The only interesting place in the stretch below is Mongewell, where a large piece of artificial water joins the river, and near it is a small church quaintly built. Shute Barrington, the well-known Bishop of Durham, married for his second wife the heiress of Mongewell, and lived here before his death. Below Mongewell is a long, dull stretch, good for boating, but too unshaded and open to be pleasant for loiterers. The Trial Eights take place here in December.

STREATLEY MILL

CHAPTER VI

TWIN VILLAGES

WHEN two villages stand facing one another across a bridge, it is inevitable that comparisons, however impertinent, will be made. And it may be said at once that Streatley, for all its old church, its pretty hotel, and its mill, cannot dispute the palm with Goring, which has an older church and a more charming mill, and many other advantages. Streatley church is singularly vivid in colouring. Rarely is there to be seen a deeper green-gold than that made by the lichen on the red roof, and when the sunshine flashes out upon it the effect is positively startling.

Not less attractive in its way is the red-roofed hotel with its backing of thick, green foliage, its tiny grass plots on the river's edge, and its gay flowers. The flour mill would be a valuable asset in the beauty items of any place not eclipsed by so near a neighbour.

There are islands in the stream, and the bridge which runs across them is singularly picturesque. This is one of the few old wooden bridges remaining, and it is doubtless destined soon to be replaced by one of iron, as has been done at Pangbourne. At this one can hardly cavil, for delightful as are the long slender wooden piles to look at, they do seem as if they might give way unexpectedly at any minute.

If we stand down by the lock there are numberless views in all directions, each good in itself. It is a hot day in summer, and the vivid scarlet and the deep carmine of the lock-keeper's geraniums literally strike one's eyeballs with their colour. We do not, alas! hear the wash of the water tumbling over the weir, for weirs in summer often run dry, or give only a small trickle, though it is

STREATLEY

just the time when their gay music would most appeal to the heart of man. The lock-keeper has stories to tell of the days before the "pound" locks, as they used to be called, were made. What we call the weirs were then the "locks." The great barges had to be towed up the weirs by means of rope and capstan; and sometimes, when the water ran low, they had to wait for weeks for a freshet that would enable them to get up. The lock here is only five-eighths of a mile below that at Cleeve, and these two are the nearest together on the river, except those of Temple and Hurley. Beyond Cleeve there is a long stretch of six and a-half miles before the next, Benson Lock. It almost seems as if the powers that deal with locks had in their justice tried to make things even by multiplying them in the beauty spots, so that those who want only the best have to pay for it by the worry of passing locks; while those who are content with something less can have it without bother. Some locks, however, have been done away with as unnecessary. There used to be one between those of Cleeve and Benson, and another at Hartslock Wood, below Goring; but these have disappeared.

The ancient road known as the Icknield Street

crosses the river at Streatley; it was used by the Romans, but made long before their time.

High beyond the bridge, and, rising above it, as we stand at the lock, is the grand sweep of hill locally known as Greenhill, in distinction from Whitehill on the Goring side.

To the right, on the top of the heights, are the golf links, and the small white road winds steeply up, carrying with it a touch of melancholy, which the sight of a far-away and steep road always gives, a suggestion of a journey that winds "uphill all the way."

Reading has now established a regatta to keep its own folk in its own neighbourhood on the August Bank-Holiday; and a great boon this has been to the quiet up-river places, for they are not now invaded by launches full of rollicking, bottle-shying crowds, such as are characteristic of the neighbourhood of all great towns, and on these occasions apt to become remarkably prominent.

Goring stands high among Thames villages, literally and figuratively. Its main street runs winding up-hill to the station, and though there are few of the genuine old cottages left, the small houses which have replaced them have been mostly built in the best modern river style, with exterior

GORING CHURCH

beams, porches, projecting windows and ornamental gables. Creepers flourish abundantly. From the river the church is easily seen. A small and narrow backwater leads under a bridge to within fifty yards of the tower.

The building is very old, and was originally the church of the Augustinian priory. It is partly covered with rough stucco, which is peeling off untidily in patches. The tower is Norman, and has a bastion turret, which greatly adds to its appearance, and, what is more uncommon, the east end is an apse, though we are bound in honesty to say an apse rebuilt.

Close by the church is the mill, which eclipses that at Streatley in appearance, and shows adaptability in applying its power as an electric generating station, while Streatley remains conservative, and still grinds the sweet-scented white flour. But the electric charging has not spoilt the mossy roof, gleaming green and russet alternately, or the pretty pigeon-house from which flocks of white pigeons often sweep round over the glistening water and the low islands. A very large and neat boat-house lies below the bridge on the Goring side.

Between this and Pangbourne we have at first rich well-covered heights on the one side, and high, open chalky hills on the other, dotted with the neat circular clumps usually associated with chalk uplands. But after a while these are replaced by the famous Hartslock Woods.

Speaking of the valley of the Thames between Goring and Henley, in his introduction to the *Flora of Oxfordshire*, Mr. G. Claridge Druce says:

" We may wander for miles through verdant alleys whose groundwork begins in early spring with the glossy gold of the smaller celandine, followed by the pale stars of the wood anemones and myriads of primroses, these giving place to sheets of hyacinths, 'that seem the heavens upbreaking through the earth,' the blue being here and there relieved by the yellow archangel or brightened with stitchwort; still later on the bluebells are replaced by masses of the fragrant woodruff, and these by the more sombre colouring of the bugle. Then come the creamy-white flowers of the helleborine, the dull, livid spikes of the bird's nest orchis and the blue forget-me-nots, giving place to a galaxy of summer flowers, brightening in later months into the brilliant yellow of the ragworts and the purple of the foxgloves. The grassy downs, too, in spring are resplendent with the milkwort in all its purity of colour, whether of that typical blue

which rivals the Swiss gentian in beauty, or fading
into white or blushing to pink; while mixed with
it are brilliant patches of rich orange yellow hippo-
crepis. Later on appear the rosy crimson spikes of
the pyramidal orchis and the pale lemon flowers
of lady's fingers, and the drooping blue-flowered
campanula. If perchance the land have remained
fallow, the bright flowers of iberis, sometimes suf-
fused with rich purple, the glaucous foliage of rare
fumarias, the deep crimson petals of the hybrid
poppy, the bright rosy pink spikes of sainfoin and
yellow toad flax, combine to form a varied show."

Before reaching Pangbourne we pass acres of
osier beds on the right. Pangbourne and Whitchurch stand to each other in the same relation
as do Goring and Streatley, but in this case it is
the southern side to which the palm must be
awarded. At Pangbourne the old wooden bridge has
given place to an iron one, but the deed has been
carried out in a manner that reflects credit on the
doer, for the new bridge runs in a graceful curve,
and its sides of latticed ironwork are painted white.
Seen in glimpses between the islands, the new
bridge does not detract from the charms of Pangbourne, but rather adds to them.

There are numbers of islands at Pangbourne,

and they lie in a great basin between and beneath the weirs, which are small and frequent. The pool is full of beauty. The trees grow freshly and well, and throw a veil of tender green over the water, which is, on a summer day, brilliant in hues of blue and green, cobalt, sea-green, pale apple, indigo; these can all be traced lying in strips and sections where the riotous torrent from the weirs frays out its inquietude and loses itself. In one corner by a pretty cottage is a splash of vivid crimson, an arcade of roses. Near the bridge great launch works are a blot and an eyesore, but it is so seldom we find our ointment without the proverbial fly.

Pangbourne village is quaint and pleasing enough, but it is not so beautiful as some of the villages along the Thames side. No village built haphazard, with a little river bridged over in its main street, with a brick-towered church, with dark evergreens, and a fair amount of creepers, could fail to be attractive in some sense. But there is too much new brick in Pangbourne. The river Pang is a tiny streamlet, and the winding ways do not hold that charm which can be felt even as one races by in a motor. Further up the river a row of neatly-built, red-brick and white-balconied

PANGBOURNE FROM THE SWAN HOTEL

WHITCHURCH LOCK

houses stands up against a high chalk bank over-
looking the river ; behind this, in a deep cutting,
runs the railway line. Above the bridge there is
a landing on the Whitchurch side close to the
church, which is a well-kept flint building. In the
chancel there is a monument to the Lybbe family,
dated 1599. Whitchurch is mostly built of red
brick, and is neat and clean, but without any very
great attractions. Before reaching Mapledurham
a fine old house, Hardwicke, is passed. Charles I.
stayed here and played bowls. The house itself
is well protected by trees, but it stands in rather
open country, amid bare chalk uplands, where
sometimes may be seen a curious opaline glow in
pale sunshine.

Mapledurham is greatly spoilt by the churlishness
of its main landlord. The lock-keeper is strictly forbidden to ferry anyone across the river, and though
the crossing would be but short, and would involve
only a walk of a few seconds along the bank to the
mill, it is not permitted. As the nearest bridges
on each side are those of Pangbourne and Caversham, it is necessary for anyone going by road to
keep to the north side of the river between these
points if he wants to see Mapledurham. The
place certainly is worth some trouble, but it is

small, and the restrictions are tiresome. The fine old Elizabethan house is a real mansion of the good old sort; one could imagine endless stories of romance connected with it. It was fortified during the civil wars by Sir Arthur Blount, governor of Reading, and is still held by the same family. The principal entrance is by an avenue of elms nearly a mile long, but the house is perhaps best seen through the gates from the churchyard. The church is small, and Perpendicular in style, with the exception of the tower, a modern addition in flint and brick. There is within a Blount chapel with many family memorials, including an altar-tomb.

The mill at Mapledurham is also a great delight to look upon, and numbers of artists sketch it from every point of view. The islands lying in the swirl of the weir-pool afford many a quiet nook in which to anchor, though landing is forbidden. From this it may be judged that if Mapledurham is a Paradise, it is sternly guarded with notices, which meet one on every side with the persistence of the flaming sword.

MAPLEDURHAM MILL

CHAPTER VII

A MITRED ABBOT

The Abbot of Reading was, like the Abbot of Abingdon, mitred, and bore powerful rule. Reading ranked third among the abbeys of England, and held the great privilege of coining. It was founded in 1121 by King Henry I. himself, who was afterwards buried here. It was for long supposed that Adeliza his queen lay here also, but the evidence goes to show she was buried in Flanders. The Empress Maud lies at Reading. The great church was dedicated by Thomas à Becket, and in it took place the marriage of John of Gaunt.

Fuller, who is always worth quoting, says that

though Ely "bare away the bell for bountefull feast making," Reading "spurred up close" to it, and continues: "The mention of Reading minds me of a pleasant and true story, which, to refresh my wearied self and reader, after long pains, I here intend to relate":

"King Henry VIII. as he was hunting in Windsor forest lost himself, and struck down about dinner-time to the Abbey of Reading, where, disguising himself, he was invited to the abbot's table and passed for one of the king's guard. A sirloin of beef was set before him on which the king laid on lustily, not disgracing one of that place for whom he was mistaken. 'Well fare thy heart,' quoth the abbot, 'and here in a cup of sack, I remember the health of his Grace your master. I would give a hundred pounds on the condition I could feed so heartily on beef as you do. Alas, my weak and squeasy stomach will hardly digest the wing of a small rabbit or chicken.' The king pleasantly pledged him, and heartily thanking him for his good cheer, after dinner departed as undiscovered as he came thither. Some weeks after the abbot was sent for by a pursuivant, brought up to London, clapped in the Tower, kept close prisoner, fed for a short time with bread and water. Yet

not so empty his body of food as his mind was filled
with fears, creating many suspicions to himself,
when and how he had incurred the king's displeasure. At last a sirloin of beef was set before
him, on which the abbot fed as the farmer of his
grange, and verified the proverb that 'Two hungry
meals make the third a glutton.' In springs
King Henry out of a private lobby where he
had placed himself, the invisible spectator of the
abbot's behaviour. 'My lord,' quoth the king,
'presently deposit your hundred pounds in gold,
or else no going hence all the days of your life.
I have been your physician to cure you of your
squeasy stomach, and here, as I deserve, I demand
my fee for the same.' The abbot down with his dust,
and glad he had escaped so, returned to Reading,
as somewhat lighter in purse, so much more
merrier in heart than when he came thence."

When the Dissolution came, the abbot, full of
belief in his own strength, defied the king,
though he saw the whirlwind around him which
had devastated other monasteries no less powerful
than his own. There was no over-tenderness in
Henry's methods, and Hugh Faringford, thirty-first
was abbot, hanged, drawn and quartered in front
of his own gateway in 1539.

There is very little left of this famous abbey now, and the gateway has been so carefully "restored" that there is more restoration about it than anything else; in fact, it is simply a reconstruction. Nearly all the remains lie within a very few acres, and the Forbury public garden is on the site of one of the courts of the abbey. The ruins at the east end are heavily covered with masses of ivy, but preserve the outlines of the chapter house and church, which was over five hundred feet in length.

Reading possessed a castle as well as an abbey, and the castle has vanished still more completely, leaving even its exact site unknown, though it is supposed to have been at the west end of the present Castle Street, or at the place where the prison now stands.

In 871 the Danes got as far up the river as Reading, and seized both town and castle. Many times has parliament been held in the ancient town, and many sovereigns have visited Reading, including Queen Elizabeth, who stayed there no less than six times. In the civil wars Reading was a stronghold for the king until, after a severe siege, in 1653 the garrison capitulated on condition of being allowed to walk out free with arms and baggage, a boon which was granted. After this the

CAVERSHAM

place was held by the Parliamentarians, but was again occupied for the king, only to become once again the headquarters of the Parliamentary army, and so it had many changes of fortune. St. Giles's church still bears the marks of the artillery from which it suffered during those uncertain times. There are other churches in Reading, but this is not a guide book, so there is no need to enumerate them. Archbishop Laud was born in Reading, and educated at the Free School. Reading is not actually on the river, and Caversham may be called its river-suburb. It is not a place which much attracts boating men. From its size, its manufactories, its chimneys, it is necessarily in many aspects unpleasant to those who have come to seek their rest and pleasure far from smoke and toil. The most important industries are Messrs. Sutton's seed emporium, and Messrs. Huntley and Palmer's biscuit factory, which employs more than five thousand persons; there are also breweries and many lesser works. Did it not lie between two such pre-eminently charming places as Sonning and Mapledurham, boating people would avoid it altogether.

CHAPTER VIII

SONNING AND ITS ROSES

THERE are certain notable details of the river - side which stand out in the mind after the rest have been merged in mere general remembrance of lazy happiness. In these we may include the back-water at Sutton Courtney, the woods at Clieveden, the Mill at Mapledurham, and the Rose Garden at Sonning. Roses grow well all along by the river, but nowhere so well as they do at Sonning, and the rose garden forms an attraction which draws hundreds

THE ROSE GARDEN AT SONNING

to the place.   Yet Sonning has other attractions too ; it is very varied and very pretty. When one arrives at it first, perhaps coming upstream, one is rather perplexed to discover the exact topography.   We round a great curve which encloses an osier bed ; here, in early spring, the osiers may be seen lying in great bundles, shaded from olive-green to brown madder.   Then we see some green lawns and landing places beneath the shadow of a fine clump of elms, and catch sight of the lovable old red-brick bridge, with its high centre arch, spanning the stream.   But there is another bridge, a wooden foot-bridge, which also spans the stream, at right angles to the other, and peering through beneath this, we can see the continuation of the red brick one in a new iron structure, which stretches on right up to the neat flower beds of the French Horn Hotel.   The truth is, the river suddenly widens out here into a great bulge, and in the bulge are several islands, on one of which are a mill and a house and several other things, not to forget a charming garden.   It is the river channel between this island and the bank that the first bridge, the old one, spans.   And what a view it is ! Above the bridge can be seen rising the little grey church tower.   On one side is the White Hart

8

Hotel, with its warm tone of yellow wash, its red tiles and its creepers, and above all its famous rose garden.   In the foreground is a willow-covered ait placed in exactly the right position.   It is a perfect picture.   But yet this is not the best side of the bridge.   The other side is better; for here, to resist the flow of the current, the builders placed the buttresses which emphasise the height of that centre arch; buttresses now capped with tufty grass and emerald moss, and from the crevices of which spring clumps of yellow daisies, candytuft, wallflower, hart's-tongue fern, and other things.   In the bricks all colours may be seen, after the manner of worn bricks, not even excluding blue.   The mill is, as it should be, wooden, and with Sandford Mill, is mentioned in Domesday Book.   From the dark shadow beneath its wheel, the largest on the river, gurgles away the water in cool green streams, passing beneath the overhanging boughs of planes and horse-chestnuts.   From the mighty sweep of the wheel, as it may be seen in its house, the drops rise glittering in cascades to varying heights like the sprays of diamonds on a tiara.   The mill-house, called Aberlash, stands not far off on the same island, with a delightful garden.

This island spreads onward with green lawns in a

sweeping semicircle to the lock and cottage, and from two small weirs the water dances down, adding variety to a beautiful pool where stand many irregular pollard willows on tiny aits. Over the smaller weir, framed in a setting of evergreens, is a bit of far distant blue landscape. There is a bank here too, an embankment, which might be covered with flowers according to its owner's design, but that the water nymphs, intolerant of flowers, except those of their own choosing, take a wicked delight in sweeping down over the weir, and sending the water flowing like a lace shawl all over the embankment to carry back all the roots and bulbs and other things that may have been planted there to use as playthings; their gurgle of delight at their own unending joke may be heard all day long.

The shy kingfishers love the big pool below the weir, but it is not often they are seen unless the watcher has the faculty for making himself invisible against his background and is able to remain motionless.

The woods of the Holme Park, rising high close by, throw a deep-toned shadow on the picture, particularly refreshing on a baking summer's day. Many birds find their refuge in these woods, and at night the weird cries of the owls sound hauntingly over the flats. A ghost is supposed to inhabit the park, and the owl's cry might very well serve for a ghost's moan on occasion.

Having thus explored the puzzling bit of river, we may land and walk up through the Rose Garden, or, according to Mr. Ashby Sterry in his *Lays of a Lazy Minstrel:*

> Let's land at the lawn of the cheery White Hart,
> Now gay with the glamour of June!
> For here we can lunch to the music of trees,
> In sight of the swift river running,
> Off cuts of cold beef and a prime Cheddar cheese,
> And a tankard of bitter at Sonning.

For the sake of those who have gardens of their own, we give a list of the principal roses grown at Sonning:

Monsieur E. Y. Teas, Madame Marie les Dier, Marie Baumann, Viscountess Folkestone, Duchess of Bedford, Aimée Vibert, Prince Camille de Rohan, W. A. Richardson, Edouard Morren, Queen of Queens, Sultan of Zanzibar, Suzanne M. Rodocanachi, Madame de Watteville, Souvenir d'un Ami, Homer, Duke of Teck, Duke of Edinburgh, Cristal, Jules Margottin, Mavourneen, Rêve d'Or, Clio, Countess of Rosebery, The Bourbon, Souvenir de la Malmaison, Maréchal Niel, Alfred Colombo, Mrs. W. J. Grant, Magna Charta, La France, Prince Arthur, Charles Lefebvre, Dean Hole, Mrs. F. Laing, Maman Cochet, Madame Willinoz, Horace Vernet, Caroline Testout, Gloire de Dijon, Auguste Rigstard, Abel Carrière, Abel Grand,

SONNING

Eclair, Rubens, Bessie Brown, Beauty of Waltham, Boule de
Neige, Jeremiah Dickson, Catherine Mermet, Gruss an
Teplitz, Lady Battersea.

With this brilliant mass of colour, the rich dark
reds, the glorious pinks, the pale yellows, dead
whites and the flaming apricot of William Allen
Richardson, the effect may be imagined; and the
entry to all this beauty is beneath a trellised arch
covered with masses of the Crimson Rambler!

Sonning village itself is very irregular, uphill and
downhill, with roads all ways. There are rights of
way through the quiet churchyard, where there is
a row of magnificent elms, and the villagers are
real flower lovers. Almost at any season of the
year at which flowers will flourish out of doors,
flowers there are to be seen. Earliest of all, the
quince, the yellow jasmine, and the dainty almond
blossom; then the golden bunches of laburnum
and the fresh mauve lilac; later on roses of all
kinds, not always climbing, but in bushes and
clumps. Window boxes are seen everywhere, and
Virginia creeper and ampelopsis cover up all bare
corners. The houses themselves are charming.
There are many more cottages in the older style
than can be found at Wargrave. Many a tiny
diamond-paned window is seen high up, almost lost

in a straggling creeper. The projecting storeys, the brown lathes imbedded deep in the brick, making rectangles of broken colour, the yellow wash of a deep umber, the high external chimneys, all make up many nooks to be looked at again and again with appreciation. Sydney Smith was staying at Sonning in 1807, and we can but admire his taste.

There is a tradition, very hazy, that Sonning was once the seat of a bishopric. There is no evidence at all as to this, but the fact that the See of Salisbury has held the manor since the time when Domesday Book was made may have led to the error.

The bishops had a house here, and it was at the bishops' house that King John stayed for six days a month before his death. Leland says: " And yet remaineth a faire olde House there of stone, even by the Tamise Ripe longging to the Bishop of Saresbyri, and thereby is a fine Park."

The oldest parts of the church probably date from 1180, but there is very little of this date left. The principal bits are the south doorway and a small window above it. The south aisle was built about 1350, the piers of the nave about 1400, at which date the chancel was added. The north chancel aisle and the north aisle came about 100 years later. The whole church was restored in 1852. There are one or two interesting monuments to be seen in it, and it is a good model of what a well-preserved, dignified parish church should be.

CHAPTER IX

WARGRAVE AND NEIGHBOURHOOD

WARGRAVE is one of the most delightful of
Thames-side villages. There is not much that is
old among the houses that line the village street;
thatch has almost gone. Wooden beams are not
noticeable, except when used in the modern
architecture that imitates the old; the material
seen everywhere is red brick. Wind and weather,
however, soon tone down the asperities of red brick,

THE CHURCH AT WARGRAVE

and from the rich soil creepers spring up quickly
to cover it with loving tendrils; so the street
becomes a delightful medley of casement windows,
gable ends, and bushy foliage. Not the least of
the charm is that each small house has its own
ideas about frontage, and entirely refuses to stand
in line with the rest. There are houses with their
doorsteps in the roadway, and houses modestly
retiring behind bushes in their strip of garden.
Here is a wistaria with a stem as thick as a
man's arm, and there roses and sweetbriar, purple
clematis and starry jasmine, succeeding and inter-
mingling. Wargrave has learnt to choose the
good and refuse the evil of the modern spirit;
she is clean and self-respecting as some villages
will never learn to be. Her small shops are good
of their kind, but self-conscious she is not, or
garish, or any other of the horrible things associated
with modernity.

The place centres about cross roads, but straggles
in many directions, and on the high ground
surrounding it many a new house has been built
lately, and stands amid delightful grounds.

The church, which is near the open green,
where grow fine trees, is of flint, with a red-brick
pinnacled tower, half ivy-covered. In the church

is buried Thomas Day, author of *Sandford and Merton*, who was killed by a fall from his horse in 1789. A Norman doorway, a carved oak pulpit black with age, and a huge family pew, tell of long survival, and give the church the same touch of self-respecting dignity that the village has. It can be seen from the water, peeping over greenery near a backwater, with its tower over-topped by trees.

The whole of Wargrave is seen to advantage from the water or from the meadows opposite. Many green lawns slope down to the brink, and the height of the bushy elms is a thing to note. A few Lombardy poplars break the fulness of the bosky foliage with their elongated ovals, and that most graceful of all trees, the wych elm, curves his beautiful lines in soft arches over the velvety lawns or smoothly-flowing water.

> Witch elms that counterchange the floor
>   Of this flat lawn with dusk and bright;
>   And thou, with all thy breadth and height
> Of foliage, towering sycamore.
>   —*Tennyson.*

The river turns almost a right angle at Wargrave, and, from running eastward, goes due north. The little village, being situated at the bend, gets the benefit of both vistas. The George Hotel, indeed, stands exactly at the angle, and the sweep of the water catches its wharf with full force. It boasts a signboard painted by two R.A.s; this is preserved indoors, while another swings as its proxy in the village street. Placed as it is in regard to the river channel, and with the wide flats of Shiplake meadows opposite, the hotel is exposed, and the very openness of its garden, an attraction which draws hundreds of summer visitors, makes it a butt for the racing winds of early spring. It is a pretty hotel built of brick, with a white painted verandah, after the usual river pattern; and a gigantic wistaria embowers all the front in its delicate mauve in summer, while roses trained over trellis work flash answering colour signals.

The view over the river includes the glowing sunsets, which leave a slowly dying splendour behind a distant bank of trees.

> And there was still, where day had set,
> A flush that spoke him loth to die;
> A last link of his glory yet
> Binding together earth and sky.
>   —*Moore.*

Looking up to the left is the railway bridge, which is not so ugly as it might be; below, every hundred yards shows fresh beauties.

Wargrave backwater is one of the most noted on the river, and in summer, or early spring, is a fairyland of greenery. The entrance is behind the large willow-covered island that lies below the hotel. The tiny arched bridge, not far in, is so low that one has to lie full length in a boat in order to pass under it. This is called Fiddler's bridge, though no local tradition keeps alive the origin of the name. The gentle light shimmers down between the spear-leaved willows in a veil of glory, and the stream is so narrow, one can almost touch the banks with both hands at once. In the main stream meantime, there are several islands decorated with the new rough stuccoed houses now so popular in river architecture, and, at the end where the backwater emerges again, there is a brightly-coloured boat-house. Beyond this, again, is a long stretch where there are generally house-boats. In winter, a little creek on the left bank is a kind of storehouse for them. This is a fine wide reach, and above it rises Wargrave Hill with its large white house conspicuously placed.

Further down, the river makes a succession of curves; and facing up stream is Bolney Court, in a solid, old-fashioned style, of a dull yellow colour,

while, behind and around it, the deep blue-green
of Scotch firs is seen among the lighter foliage,
and on the curving heights which block the vista
to the north, the heights above Henley, these
trees are conspicuous everywhere. Indeed, evergreens of all kinds flourish well in the chalky
soil about Wargrave.

The late C. J. Cornish said somewhere that
Thames eyots always seem to have been put in
place by a landscape gardener, and those about
Bolney recall the words. They are thickly grown
over by sedge and osiers, and overshadowed by taller
trees; between them, the channels of shining water,
half hidden half revealed, gain all the charm of
elusiveness. Has anyone ever reflected what a
kindly thought it was of Nature's, to arrange
that trees growing on the water's edge should
invariably take an outward angle, so as to lean
over the water? How much less effective the
result would have been had they grown inward,
may be pictured by imagining a river without
reflections. In the stillness of a backwater, or
in the narrowed channel beside a large island,
the beautiful effect of this outward angle is
best seen. If the channel be very narrow, the
trunks fold one behind the other in perspective,

so as to form an arch over a shining aisle. In
the water, all the many-coloured gnarled stems
are smoothed by the gentle movement into something softer than the rigid reality, with its hard
knots of shadow. The different colouring on
the stems of the same species of tree is a thing
to marvel at. From the deep mahogany of a joint
where the damp has made an open wound, to
the faint biscuit-colour of the place where a strip
of bark has been newly peeled off, the stems of
pollarded willows furnish every brown and yellow
on a painter's palette. Many of them are richly
crowned by a head of ivy, whose satin-smooth leaves
fall in garlands like locks, and sway with every
touch of air. These are reflected in the water
as a shaded mass of green with no detail.

There are so many varieties of willow that it
is difficult for the lay mind to remember them
all, and numbers of them are to be seen about
Wargrave. It is the Crack willow and the White
willow, with long slender leaves, that are commonly
pollarded as osiers, though they will grow tall
enough if they are allowed to. There is a legend
that the mournful droop of the leaves of the
weeping willow is a reminiscence of the sad time
of the Captivity:

By the waters of Babylon we sat down and wept, when we
remembered thee, O Sion ;

As for our harps, we hanged them up upon the willow trees
that grow therein.

Besides the willows, there are their cousins, the
poplars, chief among which, is the fine Populus
tremula, whose leaves whisper perpetual secrets,
even on the stillest days. This is caused by the
broad leaves being attached to a slender flattened
stalk. They are silky on the wrong side, and when
the wind blows through the foliage it turns a soft
greyish white, like a cottony mass. There is a
legend that the wood of this tree was used for
the Cross, and that in consequence it has trembled
ever since, and so its leaves are in a perpetual state
of quivering,

The poplar, like the ash, is not kind to
neighbouring trees, its numerous suckers taking
more than their share of nourishment and moisture
from the ground, and the leaves, when they fall,
seem to be as destructive as those of the beech,
for grass will not grow where they lie.

In spring, these trees shed their long catkins,
like hairy caterpillars, all over the water, and
they are swept up in heaps into every eddy.

In spite of the delights of summer, there is a

time which well bears comparison with it; I mean
the first fine days of early spring, before the rest
of the world has awakened to the fact that winter
is over. And about Wargrave at such times there
is to be found great charm by those whose senses
are alert. It is true that the splendid hedge
that lines the tow-path shows only the long
withes of the creepers and no starry flowers; that
the graceful sprays of the wild rose now appear
barbed and polished and ferocious, instead of
sweet and enticing. A bush of barberry or
berberis is not often seen in hedges, for the old
folk-lore taught that wheat never throve when
the barberry was in the hedge; therefore the
farmers grubbed it up whenever they found it.
But science has confirmed the empirical wisdom
of our fathers, for it was discovered that the
barberry furnishes the intermediate host for rust
in wheat. On the green river bank there are
quivering blades of tender green, but no flowers
with their umbrella heads of white, or bunchy
yellow, or pale mauve. Yet still there are
compensations. To begin with, the river itself
talks in spring as it never does in summer, and
what is better, one can hear it without the
interruption of human chatter or noise. One has

the whole stretch to one's self, and attuning one's ear to the key of that conversation, one can listen to it sucking at the bank, flop-flopping under the prow of one's punt, chuckling as it races past the pole, and, laughing a little silvery laugh of merriment, that we call rippling—a word we have learnt to adapt to our poor human attempts in the same direction. The river sprites are with us, and very busy they are—ceaselessly busy about nothing at all, and so happy in their activity that to hear them is to laugh for right good fellowship. The wind is in the water, urging them on faster and faster; each wavelet has its crest of foam, and, in the heights and hollows ahead there is every shade of green, from emerald to olive. One must be very still in order to imbibe the real spirit of the scene, for they are shy, these river nymphs, as shy as the birds and beasts that live around them, and have learned the fear of tempestuous man. A shy-bold wren, with a sudden glint of sunlight on his rich brown back, flies to the edge of the water where the punt lies drifting, and then darts back in haste to the shelter of that commanding hedge he never likes to leave. His pertness is all in his appearance; never did looks so belie a timid character!

A water-hen, startled by the sudden dip of the pole, flies out of the reeds close by, and skims in a swift low line to the islet opposite; her smooth dark body, with the elongated neck and scant tail, resembles an Eastern water skin.

There is a gentle continuous whispering among the reeds, as if they questioned themselves, with quiet disapprobation, why the river was always in such a hurry. From the field behind the hedge comes the sweet scream of a wheeling peewit, and two large wood-pigeons flap noisily from the tall trees on the island, a very picture of contented domesticity.

We slide on gently, close by the tow-path, until the tall hedge comes to an end, and the green meadows stretch right away from the lip of the river, and around them rise the tree-crowned heights in a semicircle, like the tiers of a giant amphitheatre.

Flop! A water rat dives furtively. Though called a rat, he is in reality a vole, and is almost exclusively graminivorous; in this differing from his namesake, the real rat, which also haunts river banks, especially near mills. With hoarse squawk, a wild duck rises heavily from cover, and after the first difficult spiral, wings off like an arrow, his long neck extended. It is a day of cloud and shadow, and suddenly the light breaks out on the trees ahead with a wild freshness that makes one catch one's breath. It races up stream, and the dun is turned to gold at the touch of its breath. The sweetness of early spring is in the air and in our blood; the larks feel it as they rise:

> Sounds of vernal showers
> On the twinkling grass,
> Rain-awaken'd flowers,
> All that ever was
> Joyous, and clear, and fresh, thy music doth surpass.
> —*Shelley.*

And there is a stirring of sap and juice in things—small things deep down in dark holes and corners, and in all green and growing things.

After this, how cloying the richness of summer, with its still days, its glaring reflections, the luscious foliage, and the overpowering scents—the thought of it strikes one's senses as the thought of a hothouse would strike a child of the moor and the mountain. And when we remember Wargrave regatta, with its crowded banks, its lined shores, its flags a-flutter, and its noise, we are thankful that August is afar off.

Though we have wandered down stream, the

bit above Wargrave is equally attractive. Just beyond the railway bridge the river Loddon flows into the Thames. To pass up it and its tributary, St. Patrick's stream, is no easy feat; yet by using this loop the lock may be evaded, and it is the only place on the river where such a trick is possible. It is, however, far the best to explore this by-way from the other end and to come down stream by its means. To reach it, one must go high up above the lock, beyond the last of the chain of islands which here breaks the channel, and there turn in under a small bridge, into this curious tributary, which starts from the river and returns to it again. It flows at first through wide flat meadows, and then bifurcates, one branch, blocked by a weir, communicating again with the Thames, and the other falling into the Loddon, and with it rejoining the main river.

Part of St. Patrick's stream is fringed by well-grown uniform pollard willows that hedge it like a wall. In summer, when the meadows are rich in buttercups, and the wind hums softly over the clover, bringing wafts of scent, and many a quaint weed adds its note of colour to the general harmony, it is very charming. But the most delightful feature is the growth of the

Leucojum æstivum, or summer snowflake, which
is so numerous that it is popularly known as the
Loddon lily. This is like a large snowdrop in
which several blooms spring from one head. It is
also to be found on several of the islands in the
main river near, but is not abundant there. The
Loddon itself rises far inland : Twyford gets its
name from lying near two branches, a twy-ford.
The stream is slow, and it is only the swift current
of St. Patrick that enlivens it lower down.

Above the mouth of the Loddon there lies an
interesting bit of the river. On a large island,
owned by the Corporation of London, stands the
lock-keeper's cottage, and opposite to it, on the
mainland, a delightful old mill-house with tiled
roof, and that weather-worn, rather battered
appearance, which all self-respecting mill-houses
aim at as the perfection of ripeness. The long
tongue of the lock island projects down stream
like the nose of a pike. In winter, the little
moorhens, partly tamed by hunger, and reassured
by the absence of those noisy humans who come
in such numbers in warmer weather, run about
all over it. Other things run too, all the year
round ; the lock-keeper has a fine stock of hens,
but accepts philosophically the fact that he can

never rear any chickens "because of the rats."
The rats, which are attracted by the ample stores
at the mill-house, and find such variety of
lodgings along the banks of the stream and in
the crevices of the much worn woodwork, are the
pest of these places.

The island is a popular camping ground, and
the pitches are generally secured early in the
season, having been well prepared beforehand by
being laid in sand and flints to ensure a dry
foundation. There are also a tiny bungalow, to
be had for two guineas the week, and a bathing
place available. Altogether a very attractive
island. The main stream races over the weir,
forming a wide tumbling pool below, and on the
other side of the island there is a pleasant stretch
down to the lock. These lock channels are
among some of the most charming places on
the river. They are generally very still, with the
mass of water hardly moving. On some days
every twig is reflected, and the view in this
particular one is well worth looking at, as, with
the group of the mill buildings rising high on
one side, and the cottage with its accompaniment
of standard roses on the other, there are the
elements of a most satisfactory composition.

The meadows slope down at just that angle that shows them off to the best advantage; they are dotted with fine trees and are crowned by clumps of wood, from which sounds the homely cawing of rooks. The red cows stand knee-deep in the placid water, lashing at the flies with their tails; and on the other side is a mass of greenery:

I . . . . .
Walked forth to ease my pain
Along the shore of silver streaming Thames;
Whose rutty bank, the which his river hems,
Was painted all with variable flowers,
And all the meads adorned with dainty gems
Fit to deck maidens' bowers.
    *   *   *   *
Sweet Thames! run softly till I end my song.
—*Spenser.*

Shiplake stands high above the flat meadows by the river bank. The little flint church, in which Tennyson was married, has a prettily buttressed tower, and around it grow many tall evergreens and waving trees. There are also some interesting old frescoes on the walls, two representing St. Christopher, who seems particularly appropriate in a river church. From the porch, down between two rows of shrubs, one can look on to the top of a mass of trees, which shuts out a bend of the silver river, and beyond them see the blue distance, miles and miles away. Mrs. Climenson, whose book on Shiplake was privately printed, suggests that the name originated in schiff-laacken, for the story goes that when the Danes got so far, their boats stuck on the shoals, and their commander ordered them to be burnt, to prevent a possibility of retreat.

CHAPTER X

HENLEY REGATTA

Who can ever think of Henley without its regatta? And yet Henley is very well worth thinking of at all times of the year. It is a pleasantly-built, middle-aged, red-brick town. Its history does not reach back so far as that of Abingdon or Reading. It boasts neither abbey nor cathedral. Near the esplanade above the bridge, there are one or two of the tumble-down, out-of-perpendicular style of cottages, which invariably add so much to a river scene; but the main

97

part of the town, which is, of course, of red
brick, has a homely air of the seventeenth
century about it. The solid and stately Red
Lion Hotel, close to the bridge, is one of the
most historic houses in the place. Charles I.
stayed here in 1632, when, after severe dissensions,
he was trying the method of ruling England without a Parliament, and when the terrible fate that
was to befall him had not yet "cast its shadow
before." It is doubtful if he paid his bills, for
he was in chronic want of money; but he left
a memento behind him which has more than
repaid the hotel, for it forms a perennial source of
interest. This is a large fresco painting of the
royal monogram and coat of arms over one of
the mantelpieces, and from the date it is evident it
was done at the time of this visit. It was not
discovered till 1889, having probably been hastily
concealed during the troublous days of Cromwell's
ascendency. Being on one of the principal coaching
roads, Henley received more than its share of
celebrated visitors. On July the 12th, 1788,
George III., with the Queen and three of
his daughters, had breakfast at the Red Lion;
George IV. once dined here; and the celebrated
Duke of Marlborough regularly kept a room here

RED LION HOTEL, HENLEY

that he might use it in his journeys from Blenheim; his bed is still preserved. After these associations, that of Shenstone, who wrote a poem with a diamond on a window-pane, comes as an anti-climax. The poem begins:

> To thee, fair Freedom, I retire,
> From flattery, cards, and dice, and din;
> Nor art thou found in mansions higher
> Than the low cott or humble inn.

And the last verse, which is often quoted, runs:

> Whoe'er has travell'd life's dull round,
> Whate'er his stages may have been,
> May sigh to think he still has found
> The warmest welcome at an inn.

In summer the red brick of the hotel is almost hidden by the creepers which embrace it; especially noticeable is the glorious wistaria, most lovely of all the climbing plants.

The bridge was built in 1786, and is of stone. The keystones of the central arch are adorned with sculptured masks of Thame and Isis. They were the work of Mrs. Damer, a cousin of Horace Walpole's, and as such falling within the limits of the great man's kindly appreciation. Behind the hotel and well seen from the bridge, is the church, with its four corner pinnacles.

At the time of the regatta, and for some weeks

before, it is impossible to get accommodation in the town anywhere. Of all the river regattas Henley is by far the greatest, and comes even before the Boat Race in the estimation of some people. The races used to end at the bridge, and so the lawn of the Red Lion was in the position of a favoured grand-stand, but now the winning post is a quarter of a mile short of this, opposite the last villa on the left bank. The starting point is near Temple or Regatta Island, and the reach certainly makes a fine one for the purpose. The course is railed off by piles and booms, and all the hundreds of craft which gather to the scene have to cram themselves in somehow, so as not to cause obstruction. It is well not to select an outrigged boat for such an occasion. The best and most commonly seen craft are punts, worked by means of canoe paddles; for the punts are too solid to collapse easily in the pressure that may be put upon them, and the paddles, requiring little room to work, are less dangerous to one's neighbours than poles. But all kinds of skiffs and canoes appear, and some are even bold enough to tempt fate in Canadian canoes. On a brilliant day, when the light sparkles on the water, and there is enough wind to set the pennons and streamers flying, the scene

HENLEY REGATTA

is undeniably gay and pretty. All the luncheon tents on the green lawns near form a bright adjunct. Salter and Talboys, from Oxford, and other boat-builders, have landing-stages for the week, and the various clubs entertain largely. Chief among these is the Leander, whose fine club-house is on the right bank not far from the bridge; it also has a lawn further down. Not far off are the grand-stand, the Grosvenor, and the New Oxford and Cambridge Clubs, and one large lawn is taken as a clubland *pied-à-terre* for the use of any members of London clubs in general. But beside these there are the Isthmian, Sports, and Bath Clubs on the left bank, and Phyllis Court, with smooth lawns; and then a long line of house-boats begins, continuing past Fawley Court on to Temple Island, with just one break for the lawns of the Court. Bands play, luncheons are consumed, flags flutter; everyone is gay and lively, and the scene is one that can hardly be described justly in mere word painting. At noon the first race is rowed. A bell is rung to clear the course. All sorts of boats and canoes have slipped out between the openings left for them, and they must hurry back and crush into the already tightly wedged mass; in a moment everything else is

11

forgotten in the excitement of the special event. On the last evening of the regatta there is a grand firework display and a procession of illuminated boats; and, as may very well be guessed, the real success of Henley depends greatly upon the weather, which, even in the first week of July, when it takes place, is not always kind.

As we have said, the surroundings of Henley are of a sort to attract attention, even without the additional glories of the regatta. Above the bridge is a long ait, and high on the right bank rise the woods of Park Place. Here the brilliant green of the beeches is diversified by the dark blue-greens of fir and cedar. The Place was once the residence of Frederick, Prince of Wales, and the grounds were greatly improved by Field-Marshal Conway, a cousin of Horace Walpole. A long glade is cut through the wood. It runs under a bridge made of blocks of stone taken from Reading Abbey, and over this passes the road. From the river a peep of the striking vista can be had. Higher up again is Marsh Lock.

But the influence of Henley extends down as well as up the river. Phyllis and Fawley Courts both at one time belonged to Bulstrode White-locke. Fawley was wrecked very early in the

HAMBLEDEN

civil wars; but Phyllis was strongly fortified, and some of the earthworks may still be seen. Henley was a Parliamentarian stronghold, and was annoyed by the neighbourhood of plucky little Greenlands at Hambleden, which, "for a little fort, was made very strong for the King."

It belonged in the time of the Stuarts to Sir Cope d'Oyley, who was a staunch Royalist. When he died his eldest son held Greenlands for the King, and his house was battered by the cannon of the Parliamentarians from across the water. In the nineteenth century the Rt. Hon. W. H. Smith lived here, and his widow took from the village the title he himself never lived to enjoy. In Hambleden also there is a fine old manor house, and some of the clipped yews in the gardens of private houses are very remarkable. High above the place rise the woods near Fingest and Stokenchurch. The weirs at Hambleden are the most attractive on the river. Long curved bridges run across them from shore to shore, and are open to the public as a right-of-way. The curves strike off at different angles, and every moment the point of view changes. Whether we are passing over tumbling weirs, where the water glides across long mossy planes, or over sluice-gates where it bursts

through, the enchantment is the same. Flags and
tall yellow irises and the greenest of green tufts
grow in the water and about the foundations of
the bridges. Looking back at the mill, we see it
reflected in the calm, deep water above the weirs
as in a polished looking-glass. There are old cedars
and red-roofed cottages, and plenty of Scotch firs
and yew hedges in the background. Away up the
river is the white mass of Greenlands with its
pierced look-out tower.

CHAPTER XI

THE ROMANCE OF BISHAM AND HURLEY

ONE of the greatest calumnies I ever heard expressed was the remark, "What, writing a book about the river! Why, the river is all alike, isn't it?" It is true that many reaches of the river are so exceedingly attractive that there is a danger of applying the adjectives "pretty" and "beautiful" and "charming" to many of them, but the sameness is not in the reaches, it is in the poverty of one's own language. What can be more different, for instance, than the river about Maidenhead and the river above Marlow? Yet both are delightful. The patrons of the Maidenhead part no doubt outnumber those of Bisham and Hurley, but that is because Maidenhead is one of the most accessible places on the river. The station at Marlow is on a branch, and many a weary hour must be spent waiting, if one is dependent on trains. This is the only station for Hurley and Bisham, unless we go on equally far in the other direction to Henley. However, this is one of the reasons why the Marlow section is preferable to the Maidenhead one—when you do get there.

Great Marlow itself is a fairly important place for a riverside village. It is like a little country town, and though many new red-brick villas are springing up, it could not be called "residential" in the way that the word could be applied to Richmond, for instance. The ground plan is very simple. One wide street runs straight down to the bridge, and another street crosses it at the top. In the latter is to be found Marlow's chief literary association, for here still stands the cottage where Shelley lived. It is marked by a tablet, and is a low, long building, creeper-covered, and is now divided into several cottages. Here he wrote

GENERAL VIEW OF MARLOW

The Revolt of Islam and *Alastor, or the Spirit of Solitude.*

Down by the water side the whole aspect of Marlow is bright and open. It must be entirely different from the older Marlow, when the wooden bridge—which crossed the river lower down than the present one—and the old church were still in existence. At present, in the summer all is gay and clean looking. The suspension bridge, which is the best of the modern sort of bridges from an artist's point of view, is rather low over the water; standing on it one can look right down on to the green lawn of the Compleat Angler Hotel, and see the many-coloured muslins, the white flannels, the gay cushions, the awnings, and the sunshades, as if they were all a gigantic flower bed. The red hotel itself is from this point caught against the background of the Quarry Woods. Opposite to it is the very green strip of the churchyard coming right down to the edge of the river, and only separated from it by a low stone parapet: weeping willows fling their green spray out over the water, and behind is the church. It is undeniable that the materials used in the church are distinctly ugly, but the steeple goes some way towards redeeming it, and if it can be seen silhouetted, so that the materials are lost in dimness, and only the outlines are apparent, it becomes at once more than passable. Spires are not common in Thames-side churches, which are far more often capped by rather low battlemented towers.

One of the glories of Marlow is its weir. It runs in a great semicircular sweep below the hotel; and, from a terrace there, one can look right down into the swirling water; or by coming up the backwater below in a boat, one can land at the hotel without facing the lock at all, a great advantage. The weir is in several planes, and the extended flood makes a perpetual wash, rising to a roar in winter, and dwindling to the merest tinkle in summer. Marlow is distinctly a summer place: its openness, its many trees, its wide reach of water, and the splash of the weir are all summer accompaniments; and in winter, when the wind sweeps down from the south, the unprotected side, and the water hisses and bubbles in its struggle to get down to lower levels, it is weird and melancholy.

The lock channel is fringed by several islets, and there is the usual mill, and a pretty wooden foot-bridge. Several of the most graceful of

QUARRY WOODS

our trees, the dainty silver birch, stand near the mill. On some of the lower islands osiers grow, and there are one or two neat boat-houses. Wide meadows fringe the river below; and eastward—the bridge lies due north and south—are the famous Quarry Woods, held by many to be superior even to the Clieveden Woods. In some points they are, and not the least of these is that they are traversed by several roads, while those at Clieveden are kept strictly private. The woods are composed almost wholly of beech, the tree that loves the chalk, here so abundant, and only a few patches of larch may be seen in clumps among them. Beginning at the water's edge, rising above the curious white castle with harled walls called Quarry Hill, now to let, the woods continue in a straight line inland, getting further and further from the river as they go. It is difficult to say at what season of the year they are the most beautiful. In early spring, before the buds burst, if looked at in the mass, there is to be seen a kind of purple bloom made by the myriad buds, which is not found in any mixed woods. In spring the buds burst out into that tender indescribable green, like nothing else in the world, and the new-born leaves, suspended from their dark and almost invisible twigs, are for all the world like fronds of giant maidenhair. In the autumn the whole ground is one blaze of rich burnt-sienna, a carpet of leaves laid so industriously that not a speck of the bare brown earth appears; and from this rise the stems smooth and straight, lichen-covered every one, and thus transformed to brilliant emerald. Where the light strikes through the rapidly thinning branches, they have the very glow of the stones themselves. It is an enchanted wood, and at any moment a wizard might peep out from behind one of those magic trunks.

The woods alone would be sufficient to give Marlow a high rank among river places. But all this is below the bridge, and above there is much to see. Not far off, on the right bank of the river, is Bisham, a tiny village with its church and abbey, now a dwelling house. The whole of Bisham is well worth lingering over. The cottages stand along the road in straggling fashion, old and new, and some of the gardens are bright with homely, sweet-scented flowers, among which, stocks and sweet-williams seem to be the favourites in the summer. One tumble-down row, rather off the road, is a mass of honeysuckle, and

BISHAM CHURCH

roses and ivy. The little church stands so near to the margin of the river that not a dozen yards separate its tower from the flood. A low moss-grown stone parapet edges the churchyard; over this elms dip their crooked boughs in a vain endeavour to touch the ripples as they spring playfully upward, driven by the wind. The little church has a square stone tower, wonderfully softened, so that it looks as if it must fray to powder at a touch. The brick battlements are a later addition, but the gentle river air has breathed on them so that they tone in harmoniously. Some of the windows are transition Norman. For ages the little church has stood there looking out across the water to the green flat meadows, and though it has been rebuilt and altered, there is much of it that is fairly ancient. The Hoby chapel was built about 1600, by the disconsolate widow of Sir Thomas Hoby, Ambassador to France; in it are several fine tombs, and on that of Sir Thomas, his lady, who was learned, as it was the fashion for great ladies to be in her time, wrote long inscriptions in Latin and Greek and English; the last of which ends up with:

"Give me, O God, a husband like unto Thomas,
Or else restore me to my husband Thomas!"

12

Eight years later she married again, so that she had presumably found a husband "like unto Thomas." The Hoby window in this chapel, with its coat of arms, is especially interesting, and when the morning sun streams through in tones of purple and gold upon the worn stones, the effect is striking.

There are one or two good brasses in the church, and a small monument to two children who are traditionally said to have owned Queen Elizabeth as mother !

From the reign of Edward VI. to 1780 the Hoby family held the abbey, and then it was bought by the ancestors of the present owner. It is a splendid group of masonry, and stands very effectively near the river. The tall tower, the oriel windows, and the red tints against the fine mass of greenery, make a very unusual picture. Bisham at one time belonged to the Knights Templars, who founded here a preceptory. But their Order was dissolved in the reign of Edward II. In 1338 the Earl of Salisbury established here a priory for Augustinian monks. This was twice surrendered, having been re-established after the first time. It is rather curious that the last prior, being permitted by the tenets of the Reformed

HURLEY BACKWATER

Church to marry, became the father of five daughters, each of whom married a bishop; while he himself was Bishop of St. Davids. Poor Anne of Cleves was presented with the abbey by her sometime husband the King, who, however, died before the gift was confirmed. She was allowed to retain it, and from her it passed to the Hobys as aforesaid. The house has therefore a long history, and much of the fabric is very old. One of the oldest parts is the fine entrance gateway, dating from the reign of King Stephen. The great hall is supposed to have been at one time the church of the abbey. As three Earls of Salisbury, the great "King Maker" Warwick, and Edward Plantagenet, unhappy son of an unhappy father, were all buried in the abbey church, there is every reason to suppose that their bones lie beneath the pavement in the hall.

During Queen Mary's reign Princess Elizabeth was a prisoner at Bisham under the charge of Sir Thomas Hoby. No doubt she "took water" frequently, and glided gently down with the stream; for people were accustomed to use their river when there were no roads to speak of. She must often have gazed upon the Quarry Woods in all their flaming splendour of autumn, but the Marlow she knew is so different from our Marlow we can hardly otherwise picture it. Several alterations were made at the abbey while Elizabeth was there, such as the construction of a dais, and a large window; small points, which show, however, that she was treated with all due respect. And she herself has left it on record that she received kindness and courtesy from her enforced hosts. These alterations were followed subsequently, in her own reign, by the rebuilding of much of the abbey, which was then made as we now see it.

It is inevitable that such a historic house should have a tradition or two attached to it; and traditions are not lacking. It is said that the ghost of someone drowned in the river rises at times in the form of a mist, and spreads all across the channel, and woe be to anyone who attempts to penetrate it. Another tale is that the house is haunted by a certain Lady Hoby, who beat her little boy to death because he could not write without blots. She goes about wringing her hands and trying to cleanse them from indelible inkstains. The story has probably some foundation, for a number of copybooks of the age of Elizabeth were discovered behind one of the shutters during some

BISHAM ABBEY

later alterations, and one of these was deluged in every line with blots. We all know that great severity was exercised by parents with their children at that time; even Lady Jane Grey had to undergo "pinches, nips, and bobs," until she thought herself "in hell," while with her parents, and the story, if not the ghost, may safely be accepted.

Another tradition tells of an elopement. One of the Earls of Salisbury, about to set out for the Holy Land, sent for his daughter, who was a nun at the convent of Little Marlow, to bid him farewell. She came to him at Bisham, and while there was persuaded by one of the squires to elope with him. The pair crossed the water, but were almost immediately captured. The girl was presumably returned to her nunnery, where her escapade would give her something to think of during all the monotonous days that followed, and the man was imprisoned at Bisham. In attempting to make his escape he fell from a high window and was badly injured. It is said that he afterwards took the vows and became a monk.

Temple Mill and House and Lock, which come next to Bisham up the river, recall the possession of the Knights Templars. This and Hurley Lock are the two nearest together of all on the river, and experienced oarsmen frequently catch the second one by making a dash on high days and holidays when there is likely to be a crowd and consequent delay.

Interesting as Bisham is, it is rivalled by Hurley, with its remains of the fine old mansion Lady Place.

In order to reach the lock one passes under a high wooden foot-bridge, "the marrow" to one further up. On the lock island is a large red-brick mill-house, near which stand one or two evergreens; while on an apple tree in the lock-keeper's garden is a fine growth of mistletoe, of which he is justly proud. Mistletoe grows a good deal in the valley of the Thames. It is not as a rule easily seen, owing to the foliage of the trees on which it grows; but in the winter, across the frozen meadows, against the cold white sky, it may be seen in great tufts that look like giant nests.

It is supposed that the seeds of the mistletoe in order to become fruitful must pass through the body of the missel thrush, which is extremely partial to them, and seems to be almost the only bird that will touch them, hence its name; and if, as is conjectured, the seeds cannot germinate without this process, we have the phenomenon of an animal forming the "host" for a vegetable parasite.

Beyond the lock there is a sheltered channel with the quaintest old-world flavour about it, a flavour which grows yearly more and more difficult to find as it melts away before the onward sweep of the advertising age. A strip of green turf is lined by an old brick wall with lichen and moss growing on its coping, so that when the sun catches it, it is like a ribbon of gold. Tall gate piers, crowned by stone balls, frame a bit of the excellently kept velvet lawns of Lady Place. There are many of these old piers and balls, and nearly all are overgrown with roses.

> Look to the blowing rose about us—' Lo,
> Laughing,' she says, 'into the world I blow,
> At once the silken tassel of my purse
> Tear, and its treasures on the garden throw.'
> —*Fitzgerald's Omar Khayyam.*

The splendid cedars, themselves a guarantee of age that no modern Midas can summon to deck the grounds of his new mansion; the tinkle of a cow-bell from the meadow near; and the Decorated windows of Lady Place peering over the wall; all add to the impression made by the whole. The abbey was founded in 1086 for Benedictine monks. It is interesting to note what a very great attraction water always held for monks; doubtless the necessity for Friday fish was one reason for this; but one likes to think that they also loved the river for its own sake, and that they found in the current the same sort of fascination which it holds for us now. It may be also that it was the constant gliding of the water, an emblem of their own smoothly running lives, that drew them so strongly :

> Glide gently, thus for ever glide,
>   O Thames ! that other bards may see
> As lovely visions by thy side
>   As now, fair river ! come to me.
> O glide, fair stream, for ever so,
>   Thy quiet soul on all bestowing,
> Till all our minds for ever flow
>   As thy deep waters now are flowing.
>
>   *   *   *   *
>
> How calm ! how still ! the only sound,
>   The dripping of the oar suspended !
> The evening darkness gathers round
>   By virtue's holiest powers attended.
>   —*Wordsworth.*

Of this abbey not much remains. The crypt is isolated, standing away from the remainder of the buildings, and anyone may penetrate into it. The old moat is excellently well preserved, and its circuit shows that the abbey premises must have extended over at least five acres of ground. The church, which is now the parish church, is an odd little building. It has a single aisle, and the original work is Norman, though it has been much modernised. It forms part of a courtyard or quadrangle, and faces a large, barn-like structure, which was the refectory ; in parts this is also Norman, and in it are the Decorated windows. The materials used in the construction of this refectory are most curious—brick, chalk, flint, any sort of rubble, all mixed together, and very solid. The stable is built in the same way, and it is amazing that such heterogeneous stuff should have stood the test of time. Not far off also is a dove-house of a very ancient pattern. The interior, with its cavernous gloom and the numerous holes in the chalk for the birds to nest in, is well worth looking into. Indeed, the whole of this side of the buildings— away from the river—is worth landing to see. It is all within a very few yards, and once past the modern house we find the little church with its old-fashioned wooden tower, the green with its well-grown elms, and the dove-house and stable, which combine to form a very unusual scene altogether.

Sir Richard Lovelace, created Baron Lovelace by Charles I., built Lady Place on the site of the abbey in 1600.   He was a relative of the Cavalier poet of the same name.

In Macaulay's history there is an account of Lady Place, given graphically as he well knew how.   He is speaking of a descendant of the founder, and he says:

"His mansion, built by his ancestors out of the spoils of the Spanish galleons from the Indies, rose on the ruins of a house of Our Lady in that beautiful valley, through which the Thames, not yet defiled by the precincts of a great capital, nor rising and falling with the flow and ebb of the sea, rolls under woods of beech round the gentle hills of Berkshire.   Beneath the stately saloon, adorned by Italian pencils, was a subterraneous vault in which the bones of ancient monks had sometimes been found."

The third Lord Lovelace plotted for the coming of William of Orange, and in the crypt many a secret meeting was held to arrange the details.   It is said that the actual invitation which brought the Dutchman over was signed in this low, dark vault.

Lady Place later belonged to a brother of Admiral Kempenfelt, who went down with the *Royal George.*

Certain places are frequently associated with certain seasons of the year, and to my mind at Hurley it is always summer. The smell of the new mown hay on the long island between the lock channel and part of the main stream, the faint, delicate scent of dog-roses, and all the other scents that load the summer air, seem to linger for ever in this sheltered place. The backwater running up on the other side of this island to the weir is a very enticing one. Thirsty plants dip their pretty heads to drink of the water that comes swirling from the weir like frosted glass, and trees of all sorts—ash, elm, horse-chestnut, and the ubiquitous willows and poplars—lean over the water in crooked elbows, giving a sweet shade and a delicious coolness. The weir is a long one, broken by islands into three parts. Another long island is parallel to the first one. Indeed, Hurley is a complicated place, and one that is ever new. The swans certainly appreciate it. Drayton says " Our flood's queen, Thames, with ships and swans is crowned." I don't know about the ships; nothing very large can get above Molesey Lock; but as for the swans they abound, and especially about here.

The swans on the river belong to the Crown,

the Vintners' and the Dyers' Companies. The
grant of this privilege to the companies goes
back so far that it is lost in the mists of antiquity.
The Crown is far the largest holder, but as the
numbers of swans, of course, vary from year to
year, it is difficult to form an estimate of the total.
The Vintners, who come next, own perhaps 150.
They preserve only those that live below Marsh
Lock, with the exception of a few black ones,
which, contrary to expectation, have thriven very
well, and find a happy hunting ground about
Goring and Moulsford. The system of marking,
called swan-upping, has been modified of late years,
as a protest was made against it on the ground of
cruelty. Before that time the Vintners marked
their swans with a large V right across the upper
mandible, but now they give only two little nicks,
one on each side. From this comes the well-known
sign of old yards and public-houses, the Swan with
Two Necks, a corruption of nicks! The Dyers
have a nick on one side only. The origin and
variety of swan marks is a curious subject. The
process of swan-upping, or as it is often incorrectly
called, swan-hopping, gives an occasion for a
pleasant excursion, as it occurs about a fortnight
before the August Bank-Holiday, in the very

height of the summer. Only the birds of the current year are done, as the marks generally last for life, and though they are accustomed to see too many people to fear mankind, the handling naturally frightens them. The swans, as a rule, find their own living, grubbing about in the banks and on the river bottom, and they are also occasionally fed from house-boats and pleasure boats, but in winter sometimes they are hard put to it, and provision has to be made by their owners.

A swan exercises on me something of the same fascination that a camel does; though far be it from me to compare the two in grace. They are both full of character, and both preserve a strictly critical attitude toward the human race. In the case of the swan, nature has perhaps dealt unfairly with him, for the curious little black cap, at the junction of bill and head, technically known as the " berry," gives him a fixed expression which he has no power to alter, even if he felt beaming with good humour. As it is, he is condemned to go through life as if he momentarily expected an attack upon his dignity and was prepared to repel it. When the sun is shining and the swan dips his long neck in the water and flings it upon his shoulders, the large, glistening drops, running together on the oily surface, lie like a necklet of diamonds in the hollow of his back.

The irises and bur-reeds line the low banks above the weir, and a line of short black poplars give some shade.

> And on by many a level mead,
> And shadowing bluffs that made the banks,
> We glided, winding under ranks
> Of iris and the golden reed.
>
> —*Tennyson.*

I have said that Hurley is a summer place, and so it is; but there is one spring beauty which those who know it only in summer must for ever miss. On the slopes where the heights on the northern side fold into one another there is a little pillared temple, and about and around it some lavish and generous person has planted crocuses in big battalions, and they lie there in the sun, royal in purple and gold, and quite as rich in tint as those lights shining through the stained glass window at Bisham we saw a while ago.

Above the next stretch of the river stands the great modern palace of Danesfield, which is built of chalk, one would imagine a singularly unlasting material. Though hidden by trees from directly beneath, from a distance it is very noticeable, and the white walls gleam out beneath the red tiles in a way that cannot be overlooked. It is well thus to have used local material, for local it is, as can be seen by the great chalk cliffs that line the river side; and the idea is daring and original. The interior fittings are worthy of any palace, and no pains and cost has been spared. It is a worthy object to build a house which shall rank with those bygone mansions on which their owners so lovingly lavished their thought and time, and which have also so frequently disappeared. The name arises from the fact of there having been a Danish camp in the neighbourhood, and the place is still pointed out. After this there is rather a flat bit of meadow land, fringed with sedge and many a gay plant, growing gallantly in blue and mauve. We pass two reedy islands opposite a line of little houses called Frogmill, and then we see Medmenham Abbey, which looks more imposing than it is, being at the best a carefully composed ruin. However, sometimes these compositions, if artistically done, are worth having, and Medmenham has memories behind it. It was once a real abbey, founded for Cistercian monks in 1200. But after the Dissolution the buildings fell into ruin. Later they became the headquarters of the daring and impious club known as the "Hell Fire" Club, of which one of the leading spirits was Sir Frances Dashwood, afterwards Lord Le Despencer, the same who built the church at West Wycombe, only a few miles away as the crow flies. This is a church where the pulpit and reading desk are armchairs; the latter stands on a chest of drawers, which, being pulled out, serve as steps. On the tower of the church an immense ball like a gigantic football is tethered by chains. This can contain twelve people, and the mad lord held meetings here with his friends. The motto of his club was *Fay ce que voudras*, and the members went as near to devil worship as they dared. Once while they were at Medmenham someone let a huge ape down the chimney, when the revellers, worked up to a frantic pitch of excitement and more than half drunk, thought that his Satanic majesty had paid them a visit in good earnest. From such orgies Medmenham has long been free, and it is now a respectable dwelling house with a nice bit of cloister over which ivy hangs in folds, and to which the word "picturesque" may quite fitly be applied.

There is a ferry over the river at Medmenham, and, not far off, the old Abbey Hotel, in which numbers of artists stay. Up the green lane is a

curious old house, once the residence of Sir John
Borlase, whom Charles II. used to visit, riding
here on horseback, accompanied frequently, so it is
said, by Nell Gwynne. Standing by the high
road, which here is not half a mile from the river,
is a quaint little church with wooden porch and
shady evergreens, a very model of what a tiny
village church should be.

CHAPTER XII

BOULTER'S LOCK AND MAIDENHEAD

HUMAN beings are by nature sociable; and to state that a crowd of well-dressed people will be at a certain point of the river at a particular date, is to ensure that everyone else who possibly can will be there too—only better dressed. It would seem to the ordinary ungregarious bachelor that Boulter's Lock, the Sunday after Ascot, would be a place to avoid, for there will be the necessity of waiting for hours on a river—grilling in the sun if

BOULTER'S LOCK, ASCOT SUNDAY

the day be fine, or shivering if the day be cloudy; for the English climate never lacks the spice of uncertainty, and at this season of the year it is more capricious than usual. The middle of June is proverbially a time of roses, but it is just as likely to be a time for chills, at least so says the pessimist. To the optimist and he who "loves his fellow-men," Boulter's Lock, on this one day of the year, reveals itself to memory as a day of delight and flashing colour; he has only to shut his eyes to recall a scene as brilliant as a flower garden. Here, close to him, lies a long, flat-bottomed punt, with gay cushions on which lean two fair girls, their faces toned to a pink glow by the sun's rays penetrating gently through their rose-pink sunshades. Their large flapping hats are tied under their chins with huge bows of ribbon as pink as their cheeks; their soft, white muslin dresses lie in folds and frills and heaps bewildering to contemplate; they are exactly, exasperatingly, absurdly alike. "How can a woman be such an idiot as to duplicate her charms?" the onlooker exclaims to himself; but he looks again. Dark eyes dancing as merrily as the ripples on the breeze-stirred water; chatter and laugh; and babble as soft and meaningless as the gurgle of the little tributary

14

stream ; textures of fabric as delicate as the flowers peeping over the grey stone walls from the lock-keeper's garden above ; dainty arms bare to the elbow ; Japanese umbrellas jewelled in the sunlight ; striped awnings, as gay as Joseph's coat, flapping softly ; the long low outlines of craft of every kind, skiff and dingey and canoe, from the smoothly gliding little electric launch to the heavy clinker-built boat on hire for its tenth season ; these items make up a scene quite unlike anything else. For half a mile below the lock you could step across a solid bridge of boats over half the river. Some years ago, the homely serge and sailor straw-hat were considered the proper river costume ; now, the straw is worn only by men, whose severe flannels show little alteration from year to year, for men are much more conservative in sartorial matters than women. And every tantalising muslin, lace, and flower-decked hat is considered suitable for a woman on the river. The more fantastic and enormous, the more gauzy and lace-trimmed, the better. And, as her grandmother did, the young girl dresses in the thinnest of muslins and lawns, wears an open neck in the day time, and elbow sleeves.

In pushing forward between the open lock-gates into the lock, a slender canoe fits into an almost

BELOW BOULTER'S LOCK

impossible space between the electric launch and
the punt. A heavily weighted boatload, where
four elderly women are rowed by one heated man,
falls foul of its neighbour and has to be righted.
The chatter is silenced for a moment, but rises
again when the craft are fitted, like the pieces in
an old fashioned puzzle, inside the green and slimy
walls, which throw a deep shadow on one side.
Then the gates are shut, and a wash and gurgle
of water begins, delightfully cool to hear. A
nervous girl gives a little shriek and jumps so that
every boat is set a-rocking, as all are touching.
Others laugh. It is impossible to upset, for there
is no room. The whole gently swaying mass rises
on the breast of the rising water up out of the
shadow into the sunlight; into the view of the
waiting crowds on the tow-path. Colours flash out
once more; an excited little dog rushes yapping
from stem to stern of his boat, and finally, with a
vigorous jump, lands on the lock-keeper's garden,
where there is a profusion of sweet old-fashioned
flowers, and such roses as grow nowhere but by
the river-side. Then, to the accompaniment of
the dog's frantic barks, the massive gates creak
backward on their hinges, and we ride forward
into the wide expanse of the sparkling river.

Only a few boats await the opening of the lock here, for, at this time of day, more are going up than coming down. But behind, away below the lock, a chaotic flotilla has once more collected, and may have to wait for hours, for it is rather like the process of ladling the river up in a tablespoon.

This reach at Maidenhead, is one of the most popular on the river. On each side of the wide stone bridge half a mile below the lock, Taplow and Maidenhead face one another. But though popular and easy of access, being on the Great Western Railway, which runs quick trains at frequent intervals, both stations are a little distance from the river. The name Maidenhead is derived from Maiden-hithe, or wharf, as a large wharf for wood at one time stood near the bridge. The bridge itself, though a modern fabric, is of ancient lineage, for we know that in 1352 a guild was formed for the purpose of keeping it in repair. It may be remembered that bridges at that time were considered works of charity, and competed with masses and alms as a means of doing good posthumously.

Another blissed besines is brigges to make,
   That there the pepul may not passe [*die*] after great showres,
Dole it is to drawe a deed body oute of a lake,
   That was fulled in a fount-stoon, and a felow of ours.

MAIDENHEAD

And in *Piers Plowman* :

> Therewith to build hospitals, helping the sick,
> Or roads that are rotten full rightly repair,
> Or bridges, when broken, to build up anew.

The main road between London and Bath, a well-known coaching road, runs this way, and a very good road it is. The railway bridge crosses below the road, but it is of brick with wide arches, and is by no means unsightly. Between the two is the River-side club, where a band plays on the smooth green lawn in the season, and the smartest of smart costumes are the rule. Near here also is Bond's boat-house and a willow-grown islet. There are numbers of steps and railings and landing stages, all painted white, and these give a certain lightness to the scene. Close by the bridge are several hotels, of which the oldest established is Skindle's, low-lying and creeper-covered, on the Taplow side. Boats for hire line the banks everywhere, for many cater for the wants of the butterfly visitor, out of whom enough must be taken in the season to carry the establishments on through the winter; and the river visitor is essentially a butterfly. Few know the charms of the Thames in the winter, when, in an east and west stretch, the glowing red ball of the sun sinks

behind dun banks of mist; when the trees are
leafless, and the skeleton branches are outlined
against a pale clear sky; when a touch of frost is
in the air, and the river glides so stilly that it
almost seems asleep.

> A bitter day, that early sank
> Behind a purple frosty bank
> Of vapour, leaving night forlorn.
> —*Tennyson.*

The visitor goes to the river in the summer
because of its coolness, and though the coolness is
ofttimes delusive, being in appearance rather than
reality, lying in the sight of the sparkles and the
sound of the ripples, yet it is a fine make-believe.
Such river-side hotels as cater for the season are
content to lie dormant all the chill long winter,
until, with the breath of early spring, the celandines
raise their polished golden faces and the lords and
ladies stud the hedgerows.   Then a few adventurous
beings come down on the first fine days, like the
early swallows, a portent that summer is at hand;
and these lucky people have the river largely to
themselves, and do not find lovers in every
attractive backwater; and if they have to row to
keep themselves warm, they gain an increase of
vigour that no burning summer sun can give.

The view from Maidenhead Bridge northwards—

for here the river runs due south—is spoilt by the gasometers which rise over the willow-covered islets. But once past Boulter's Lock, the scenery improves with every hundred yards. Close by the lock itself is Ray Mead Hotel, where the deep carmine-tinted geraniums grow in quantities. Sometimes as many as three hundred people are supplied with tea at the hotel on a fine summer afternoon, while over a thousand pass through the lock. Above Boulter's is a secluded backwater formed by the stream of a mill, and this is one of the pleasantest retreats in the neighbourhood.

> . . . . In my boat I lie
> Moor'd to the cool bank in the summer heats.
> —*Matthew Arnold.*

Above the river, on the east, rise the cliff-like heights of Clieveden, wooded to their summits, and seen magnificently by reason of the curve at the end of the reach, which gives their full sweep at one glance. The cliff rises to a height of 140 feet, but the thickness of the trees, and their own height towering above, make it look much higher. The trees are of all kinds, oak and beech, chestnut and ash, and many a dark evergreen; while here and there a Lombardy poplar shoots up like a straight line, and the wild clematis throws its shawls of greenery from tree to tree, giving the whole the appearance of a tropical forest. Seen in early spring, when the tender green of the beeches and the bursting gummy buds of the horse-chestnut are shedding a veil over the fretwork of twig and bough, they are glorious enough; but in autumn, when orange and russet break out in all directions, they are, perhaps, more imposing. River people do not, as a rule, see them at their best, for before that touch of frost has come which sends a flame of crimson over the maples, and heightens the orange of the beeches, the fairweather boatsman has fled to his fireside.

At one point we catch a glimpse of Clieveden itself, standing high and facing downstream. Evelyn says in his diary:

> I went to Clifden, that stupendous natural rock, wood, and prospect, of the Duke of Buckingham's, buildings of extraordinary expense. . . . The stande, somewhat like Frascati as to its front, and on the platform is a circular view to the utmost verge of the horizon, which, with the serpenting of the Thames, is admirable. . . . But the land all about wretchedly barren, and producing nothing but fern.

The taste of those days differed from ours; now we should prefer to see an expanse of ferns to a field of potatoes.

The first great mansion here was built by "Steenie," the Duke of Buckingham, King Charles's favourite. He was a villain, even for a time of slack morals, and the chief association connected with his house is that he brought here a comrade in every way suited to him, in the person of the Countess of Shrewsbury, who stood by, dressed as a page, holding his horse, while he killed her husband in a duel. The house was twice burnt down; the present one was built about the middle of the nineteenth century, and belongs to Mr. Astor. A pleasanter memory is that of the poet Thomson, whose masque *Alfred* was acted here in 1740, on the birthday of Princess Augusta. This contained, as a kernel, the song "Rule Britannia," destined to survive long after its husk had been forgotten.

Opposite Clieveden the ground is low lying, and, to use Evelyn's word, the river "serpents" a good deal. There are several islands, on one of which, called Formosa, there is a house. There are several side-streams crossed by footbridges, and in one of these is the lock. The main stream continues in a great sweep, and is guarded by two weirs. The fishing here is very popular, and though it belongs to Lord Boston, permission to fish may

be obtained by writing beforehand. Hedsor Church
stands well on high ground near; and with its
bosky foliage and many islets, the river here is not
a bad place in which to idle away many an hour.

The hotel at Cookham is right down on the
water's edge, and from its lawn a charming view is
gained of the main stream breaking into its many
channels, with the wooded island of Formosa in
the middle. All about here is a favourite place
for anglers, and many a punt is moored across
stream with its ridiculous chairs on which sit two
or three solemn elderly men, content to sit, and
sit, and watch the dull brown water rush beneath
for hour after hour, without once raising their eyes
to see the green of the witching trees, or listening
to the hum of the joyous life around them. To an
onlooker they appear to be quaffing the flattest
part of the sport, having missed all its head and
froth. How different the punt fisher's day from
that of the man who starts off up-stream, through
many a low-lying willow-fringed meadow, who
reaches over to land his fly in the deep brown pool
into which the stream falls. Punt fishing, like loch
fishing, must have its fascinations, or few would do
it, but it lacks all the sparkle expressed in such a
song as that of Walton's, for instance :

In a morning, up we rise,
 Ere Aurora's peeping,
Drink a cup to wash our eyes,
Leave the sluggard sleeping.
 Then we go
 To and fro,
 With our knacks
 At our backs,
 To such streams
 As the Thames,
If we have the leisure.

The less said about the rhyme the better, but this has the swing and lilt of the true feeling!

From Cookham Bridge we can see the gaily covered lawn of the hotel, where a perfect flotilla of craft is anchored, while the owners have tea or more cooling drinks; and turning we can view the wide expanse of Bourne End, where the races of the Upper Thames Sailing Club are held all the summer, and where, about the end of June, when the great regatta is held, the surface of the water is dotted with swan-like boats.

CHAPTER XIII

WINDSOR AND ETON

HOWEVER disappointed a foreign monarch, on his
first visit to England, may be with the drab
hideousness of Buckingham Palace, he cannot
but confess that in Windsor Castle we have a
dwelling meet even for the King of England.
Both architecturally and by reason of its age,
Windsor is a truly royal palace. Its history is
linked with that of our kings until its very
stones proclaim the annals of our country. Ages
ago, Edward the Confessor took a fancy to this

140

WINDSOR CASTLE

quiet place by the Thames, and he gave it to his beloved monks of Westminster. William I. saw what a splendid shooting lodge might be built in the midst of the wild and open country abounding in game, and after having first one shooting lodge and then another in the neighbourhood, he acquired the high outstanding boss or knob of chalk on which the castle stands, and built thereon a residence for himself. His son, Henry I., altered it greatly; and succeeding kings and queens have rarely been content to leave it without an alteration or addition as their mark. Windsor has ever been a favourite with royalty. It has held its own while Westminster and Whitehall and Greenwich utterly vanished; while the Tower and Hampton have ceased to be royal dwellings; and it is still pre-eminently the royal castle. Certain kings, such as William III., have sometimes preferred other places for a while, but Windsor has satisfied alike the dignity of Edward III. and the homeliness of George III.

The situation is superb. The castle stands high above the river, which here curves, so as to show off its irregular outlines to the greatest advantage. They rise in a series of rough levels to the mighty Round Tower, the crown of the whole, which is massive enough to dominate, but not sufficiently high to dwarf the rest. Turrets, battlements, and smaller towers serve only to emphasize the dignity of this central keep. It was built in the time of Edward III., and strangely enough, though altered and heightened in that worst period of architectural taste, the reign of George IV., it was not spoiled; and even to a child proclaims something of the grandeur one naturally associates with it.

As seen from the bridge the whole of the north range can be followed by the eye, from the Prince of Wales's Tower, facing the east terrace, to the Curfew Tower on the west. Intermediately there are the State apartments, and the Norman gateway, over which is the Library. These overlook the north terrace—open to the public at all hours from sunrise to sunset.

The view from this terrace is very fine, stretching away to Maidenhead, and at times, on days of cloud and shadow, the light-coloured walls of Clieveden stand out suddenly, caught by a passing gleam, amid a forest of green trees. We can look down on the whole of Eton—the church with its tall spire; the buttresses and pinnacles of the chapel standing up white against an indigo background; the red and blue roofs piled this way and that; and the green playing fields girdled by the swift river. It was on the castle terrace that George III. used to walk with all his family, except the erring eldest, when he took those tiresome parades which Miss Burney describes with so much life-like detail.

The Chapel cannot be seen from the river, as it is in the lower ward behind the canons' houses, and is not sufficiently high to rise well above them.

It would be of little use to attempt to tell stories of Windsor, for its history belongs to the history of England and not to the river Thames; yet there is one memory which may be noted. Young James Stuart of Scotland had been sent by his father, Robert III., to France after the death of his elder brother, the wild Duke of Rothesay, nominally for education, but in reality for safe keeping. The boy was captured by the English while on the sea and brought as a prisoner to England. He was then only about ten or twelve years old. He was treated with every consideration, and educated so worthily that he became afterwards one of the best of all the Scottish kings. He was at first in the Tower and elsewhere, but when he reached young manhood he was brought to Windsor, where he had apartments allotted to him. Though he was allowed to follow the chase and pursue the amusements of his time, he was yet a prisoner, and the sad opening stanzas of his great poem, the *Kingis Quair*, speak the melancholy he often felt. This poem was composed at Windsor, and its pensiveness changes after the day when, looking down from his window in the castle, the youth saw walking in the garden Joan Beaufort, whom he afterwards made his wife:

> And therewith cast I down mine eye again,
> Where as I saw, walking under the tower,
> The fairest or the freshest young flower
> That ever I saw methought before that hour.

His visions further on in the poem must have been coloured more or less by what he daily saw before him, and we may credit to the Thames the flowing lines:

> Where in a lusty plain took I my way,
> Along a river pleasant to behold,
> Embroidered all with fresh flowers gay,
> Where, through the gravel, bright as any gold,
> The crystal water ran so clear and cold.

Windsor should be seen in sunshine and heat, when black shadows set off the towering walls, and all the uneven houses and crooked streets

WINDSOR

are pieced in light and shade. Then it is exceedingly like a foreign town in its details; and many people who travel miles to admire Chinon, and others of its class, would do well to visit Windsor first.

The town has always been subordinate to the castle, for it was the castle that caused the town to spring up, as there were always numbers of artificers, attendants, grooms, workmen and others needed for the service of the Court. In the fourteenth century it was reckoned that the Court employed an army of 20,000 of such people. These would all have to be housed somehow, and the nearer the protection of the castle the better; hence the town on the slopes.

The Home Park, in which is the mausoleum, borders the river. It is separated by a road from the Great Park, made for hunting. Pope's poem on "Windsor Forest" is not particularly beautiful; perhaps the best descriptive lines are those that follow:

> There, interspersed in lawns and opening glades,
> Thin trees arise that shun each other's shades:
> Here in full light the russet plains extend;
> There, wrapt in clouds, the bluish hills ascend.

Windsor Park is introduced by Shakspeare as

the scene of some of Falstaff's escapades, an honour shared by the neat, bright village of Datchet, opposite. Datchet is a model village grouped about a green, and the houses are softened by all the usual creepers and bushes: we see roses, jasmine, laurustinus, magnolia, and ampelopsis at every turn. Above and below Datchet this clean neatness continues.

The Victoria and Albert bridges are severe, and the weir and the great bow of the channel, which is cut by the lock-stream, have no particular characteristics. The whole neighbourhood has rather the air of holding itself on its best behaviour, as though royalty might any moment appear upon the scene. As might be expected, the scenery is rather like the poetry it inspired. Here is Sir John Denham's effusion about Cooper's Hill :

> My eye, descending from the hill, surveys
> Where Thames, among the wanton valleys strays:
> Thames, the most loved of all the Ocean's sons
> By his old sire, to his embraces runs :
> > Hasting to pay his tribute to the sea,
> > Like mortal life to meet eternity.

There is a pretty reach below Old Windsor, where willows and poplars are massed effectively. It is in places like this, where they grow abundantly, that the beautiful tawny colour which willows assume in the spring, just before bursting into leaf, can be best seen.

The Bells of Ouseley stands at a bend, and with its tinted walls and the old elm tree growing close to the entrance, is a typical old-English Inn. The road to Staines passes by the water's edge, and the guide-post is less reticent than guide-posts are wont to be, for it tells us this is the "Way to Staines, except at high-water."

As we pass softly back up the current to Eton, we think how often in this reach the incomparable Izaak and his friend Sir Henry Wotton fished together.

> I sat down under a willow tree by the water side ... for I could there sit quietly, and, looking on the water, see some fishes sport themselves in the silver streams, others leaping at flies of several shapes and colours , ... looking down the meadows, could see here a boy gathering lilies and ladysmocks, and there a girl cropping culver-keys and cowslips.

Wotton built a fishing box a mile below the college, from which he and Walton often sallied forth during the fifteen years he was provost of Eton, and to his rod many a "jealous trout that low did lie, rose at a well dissembled fly," as he himself has left on record.

16

Ye distant spires, ye antique towers
   That crown the wat'ry glade,
Where grateful Science still adores
   Her Henry's holy shade;
And ye, that from the stately brow
Of Windsor's heights th' expanse below
Of grove, of lawn, of mead survey,
Whose turf, whose shade, whose flowers among
Wanders the hoary Thames along
   His silver-winding way.   *—Gray.*

In rounding the great sweep of the river below the London and South Western railway bridge, we catch at once the pinnacles of Eton chapel—most glorious of chapels—and see the green playing fields.

The long tree-covered island of Romney, on one side of which lies the lock, ends in a terrible "snout," strengthened by "camp-shedding." This point is locally known as the "Cobbler," and is a source of peril to many an inexperienced boatman.

The bridge over the river can, unfortunately, hardly be called a good feature in the landscape—it is as ugly as a railway bridge! Just above it is a row of boat-houses, and then follows the Brocas, the famous meadow. Above the bridge is a tiny islet which serves as an objective in the Fourth of June procession of boats. The boats come down and round the island, and once more

ETON CHAPEL FROM THE FIELDS

returning, pass under the bridge to the lock, having made a sort of spiral. Nearly all the Eton races are rowed in this strip of the river, though, of course, Henley Regatta is the greatest event in the boating calendar. A small string of islands faces some little public gardens, and away northward winds the Great Western Railway on a series of small arches which carry it over the marshy ground, no doubt at one time under water.

Beyond the line is a small backwater known as Cuckoo weir, the bathing place of the lower boys. Here the swimming trials take place, when a set of trembling pink youngsters stand in a punt ready to take a graceful header, or, from sheer nervousness, to fall with an ugly flop smack upon the water and be disqualified for the time being!

The bathing place of the upper boys, called by the dignified title of Athens, is further up in the main river, near the curious island on which is Windsor racecourse. The river winds giddily in and out between the end of this island and Upper and Lower Hope, which lie between it and Cuckoo weir. A mill stands at the end of the long narrow stream that separates the racecourse from the mainland, and on the other side of the island is Boveney Lock. The quaint old chapel stands amid trees further up.

Above the island was once Surley Hall, a favourite resort of the Etonians, but it is now pulled down, and Monkey Island is the place to go to on half-holidays. Monkey Island is a good way up, and is the third of a row of islands. The little one below it, called Queen's ait, now belongs to the Eton boys, who have built a small cottage on it. Monkey Island itself is a curious and attractive place, except when the launches come up from Windsor on Saturdays, bringing hundreds of people, who sit about at little tables on the green sward under the famous walnut trees, and call for refreshments. There is a large pavilion, part boat-house, which belongs to the Eton boys, where they can get tea served without mingling with the townspeople. Near it is a quaint little temple. This, as well as the house, now the hotel, was built by the third Duke of Marlborough, a man of curious taste. The hall in the hotel is painted all round with the figures of monkeys engaged in various sports and pastimes. There is a broad frieze which appears to have been executed in water colours on plaster; the ceiling is likewise painted, but in rather a different style. The monkeys are a good size, and attract a vast crowd of visitors. The pretty verandah round the hotel redeems its appearance externally. Inside it has at once all the attractions and disadvantages of an old house—low ceilings, very small rooms; but on the other hand there are windings and twistings, crooked passages and odd corners, that delight the heart of those to whom machine-made houses are an abomination. The duke's bedroom is shown, and is as queerly shaped a room as ever mortal man conceived. Monkey Island is being embanked with the precious gravel dredged from the bed of the Thames, and, though no doubt a necessary precaution, as the river insidiously breaks off what it can, the operation is not a beautiful one. The island is very proud of its walnut trees, and well it may be, for they are a great change after the ubiquitous willows, and their gnarled stems and fine shady leaves are just the right element in such a scene as a gay lawn covered with summer folk in summer dresses.

From Monkey Island the little church tower of Bray can be seen, but before reaching it Bray Lock has to be negotiated, and here are a long sinuous osier-covered ait and a mill, making, as usual, a convenient backwater.

Bray is truly a charming place, and one could find it in one's heart to forgive the vicar who turned his coat to keep his vicarage. The real man lived in the reign of Henry VIII. and his successors, and changed his religious practices in conformity with those of the sovereign for the time being, turning from Roman Catholic to Reformed Church, Reformed to Roman Catholic, and back once more with ease and pliability. In the ballad he is represented as living in the seventeenth century, and his gymnastics refer to the varying fortunes of the house of Stuart, and the Romish tendencies of the later kings of that house. Fuller, with his usual quaintness, remarks of him that he had seen some martyrs burnt at Windsor and "found this fire too hot for his tender temper." But one would fain believe it was not altogether cowardice, but also a love of his delightful village, that made him so amenable. The little flint and stone tower of the church peeps at the river over a splendid assortment of evergreens—laurels, holm oaks, yews, and spruce firs being particularly noticeable—and the old vicarage with this growth of sheltering trees and its smooth lawn right down to the water's edge, is certainly a place that one would think twice about before leaving. The village itself is so irregular that, tiny as it is, one may get lost in it. There are endless vistas of gable ends, of bowed timbers, of pretty porches, and worn brick softly embraced by vine or wistaria; yet even in Bray, new red brick is making its way. One of the most interesting features is the almshouses, and if one lands by the hotel, they are reached after only a few minutes' walk. The exterior is very quaint; large cylindrical yews and hollies, like roly-poly puddings on end, stand up in stubborn rank before the worn red brick. The statue of the founder, of an immaculate whiteness, with the glitter of gilt in the coat-of-arms below, just lightens the effect. Through an ancient arch one passes to the quadrangle, which is filled with tiny flower-beds, and surrounded by a low range of red brick with dormer windows. At the other side is the chapel covered with ivy, and this, with the little diamond panes and the brightness of the variegated flower-beds, is home-like and cosy. Yet it must be confessed that in his well-known picture, "The Harbour of Refuge," admittedly taken from Bray, Frederick Walker, the artist, has greatly improved the scene with artistic licence. The raised terrace at the side, the greater width of the quadrangle, the smooth green lawn and sheltering central tree in his picture, are far more harmonious and beautiful than the reality.

Bray is a very popular haunt with artists and boating people. In summer the George Hotel cannot take in all its visitors, and beds are hired all over the village, consequently, anyone wishing to spend some weeks in Bray must make arrangements well beforehand. This is not to be wondered at, because, as well as its own attractions, it is within easy reach of Maidenhead and the delights beyond, and its unspoilt quaintness makes it ideal to stay in. Long may Bray remain as it is, unaltered and a tiny village.

CHAPTER XIV

MAGNA CHARTA

MAGNA CHARTA ISLAND is something of a shock at first sight; it is so exceptionally well cared for and so pretty. One pictures a tangle of wild trees, a mass of rushes, osiers perhaps, and general grimness. The osiers are confined to a fraction of the island; on the remainder is a prettily-built house of a fair size, with the very best sort of river-lawn, on which grow various fine and regular trees. Many are the evergreens; and the bosky

155

holm oak, the dignified stone pine, and the flourishing walnut, seen in conjunction with the beautifully kept turf and bright flower-beds, are altogether unlike one's conception of the place.

It is true that, though the island has the name of it, it is now generally supposed that the actual signing of our great charter of liberties took place on the mainland. John had delayed, and played false, and postponed the issue for long, but he knew now that all was up, and he was cornered. A truce was declared, and from Windsor he agreed to meet his barons and " concede to them the laws and liberties which they asked." The fifteenth of June was fixed for the day, and Runney Mead, or Runnymede, for the place. With the barons were almost the whole of the English nobility; with John, certain ecclesiastical powers, namely, the Archbishops of Canterbury and Dublin, and seven bishops, as well as some earls and barons. It is quite obvious that the barons could have had no idea of the vast consequences of their act. They would have been astonished could they have foreseen that it would become the basis of the English constitution. They merely wanted to bind down a particular king who had outraged their liberties.

One can hardly imagine a better place for the

assembling of a great body of armed men than these meadows by the river. The land is as flat as a platform, and sheltered to the south by the heights of Cooper's Hill, which rise like the tiers in an amphitheatre. The Long Mead, with the exception of the road now running across it, must have looked very much then as it does now. Runney Mead is more altered, because it is shut in by hedges. We know not if the day were fine or overcast when the great charter was signed; but when the deed was done John, in a rage, retired to Windsor. The barons remained on the meads for about ten days, during which the place must have been like a fair.

It is very hot on this part of the river on a sunny day. The trees growing on the banks are all on the north side, and consequently give little shade. They border Ankerwyke Park, and grow so close to the water that many of their roots are in it. The swallows dart to and fro, and clouds of gnats dance like thistledown in the air. Near the banks grow many flowers. The spotted knotweed or persicaria, with its bright flesh-coloured flowers, is sometimes in water, sometimes on the land; the common forget-me-not can be seen peeping up with its bright blue eyes; the pink willow herb flourishes; and the yellow iris and the purple loosestrife are also to be seen. And when there is no wind the scent of the meadow-sweet and the dog-roses becomes almost overpowering.

Ankerwyke was once a priory. It was appropriated by Henry VIII., who is said to have carried on the courtship of Anne Boleyn under the mighty chestnuts for which it was even then famous:

> The tyrant Harry felt love's softening flame,
> And sighing breathed his Anna Boleyn's name.

A bit of doggerel just about worthy of the occasion!

A more interesting association, though one that leads us rather far from the river, is Milton's residence at Horton. He lived here with his parents for five years after leaving Cambridge, and no doubt his rambles over country which would not then be hedged in and cut up as it is now, often led him in the direction of the river. It was this scenery, noted at those deeply impressionable years, that he could still see when earthly sight was gone.

Lycidas and *Comus* were both written in the next four or five years, and in

> The willows and the hazel copses green

we have a touch of real nature breaking through the conventional allusions to vines and wild thyme; also:

Ye valleys low, where the mild whispers use
Of shades, and wanton winds, and gushing brooks,
On whose fresh lap the swart star sparely looks ,
Throw hither all your quaint, enamell'd eyes
That on the green turf suck the honied showers,
And purple all the ground with vernal flowers.
Bring the rathe primrose that forsaken dies,
The tufted crow-toe, and pale jessamine,
The white pink, and the pansy freak'd with jet,
The glowing violet,
The musk-rose, and the well-attir'd woodbine,
With cowslips wan that hang the pensive head,
And every flower that sad embroidery wears.
Bid amaranthus all his beauty shed,
And daffadillies fill their cups with tears.
—*Lycidas.*

By the rushy-fringed bank
Where grows the willow and the osier dank.

* * * *

Thus I set my printless feet
O'er the cowslip's velvet head
That bends not as I tread
—*Comus.*

Not very far below Ankerwyke, the river Coln runs into the Thames near Bell Weir Lock, and a little bit above Staines is London Stone, standing in a meadow close by the water. It marked the former jurisdiction of the Lord Mayor of London over the river, but these rights are now vested in the Thames Conservators. Staines does not make the most of itself, or sufficiently endeavour to veil those unsightlinesses incidental to a town.

The large gasometers opposite London Stone are
not the only blemishes. Standing on the bridge
and looking up-stream there are many ugly,
yellow-brick, manufacturing buildings to be seen;
while the screen of willows does not hide piles
of untidy stones, rusty old iron and other ugli-
nesses. Even the very passable island in the centre
does not atone. Down stream things are a little
better, though the want of architectural beauty in
the new church by the river and the "plastered-on"
pinnacles of the parish church are both eyesores.

From Staines, however, one may pass rapidly to
a fascinating corner at Penton Hook.

CHAPTER XV

PENTON HOOK

PENTON HOOK is quite peculiar. To a select little coterie of people it is *the* place on the river, but to hundreds of others it is not known at all. To its own manifest advantage it is off the "hard high road," and the scorchers and the bounders, and the multitude generally, fly by within a comparatively short distance, little knowing what they have missed. But one or two of the favoured few turn down to quiet little Laleham, and

161

wheeling round a corner come right on to the
tow-path by the river's brink; in a hundred yards
they are at Penton Hook. But though the Hook
is very select and highly favoured, that is not to
say it lacks population, only—it is a population
of the right sort. Little camps of charming
bungalows dot the banks both above and below
the lock. Some are built on ground leased from
the Conservancy, some on that of private owners.
To each man is allotted a strip of ground, with
so much river frontage, whereon he builds to his
own taste and fancy a little one-storeyed white-
painted house, and lays out the tiny garden from
which his own white steps reach down to the
water. Think of the joy of it! The leader in
an important case has been in a stuffy court
all day, burdened with his wig and gown, seeing
all the dust and stains of unswept corners of
human nature; accusing, with upraised finger, the
brazen witness who has just perjured himself;
dragging from that yellow-faced man the secret
he thought buried. Faugh! But the court rises;
he is away. The motor takes him down in less
than an hour. Gone are the stifling garments;
the worn and wicked faces. The dull roar of
Strand traffic is replaced by the splashing of the

water as it bounds over the weir. The freed
man tumbles into flannels and lies full length
on the green grass, smoking, with the water
flowing at his feet, or he dawdles in a boat
round the Hook, tempting the fish with all the
decoys he knows. Happy man!

The trees near the bungalows, and those that
fringe the meadows near, are not pollarded; there
is space between their tall stems. The short grass,
gemmed with pink-tipped daisies, can be seen
everywhere, and there is air, and freshness, and
openness for everyone. The white paint of the
bungalows and their neat green or pink roofs,
the rows of geraniums, roses, and other flowers
carefully kept and tended, add touches of gaiety
and brightness.

There are three weirs, for the river here makes
the neatest horse-shoe in its whole length, and
the authorities have cut through the neck of land,
so that the greater part of the stream goes rioting
and tumbling in joyous confusion beneath the great
new weir, provided with a pent-house roof, under
which it is always cool on the hottest summer day,
with transparent reflections dancing on the wall
and a ripple and splash below. The second
weir, a mere tumbling-weir, is only a few yards

away. The water does not often leap over it unless it is at flood time, when it affords a safety outlet. The third and widest is a mixture, half sluice gates and half of the tumbling kind. At one time there was no weir here, and boats could avoid the lock by navigating the Hook, but that is now no longer possible. There is one advantage in it; it keeps the Hook more secluded. The little red water-gauge house is connected by wires with Staines, and so to all the rest of England. By an automatic arrangement, the register shows simultaneously here and at the offices of the water company what depth of water there is, so that they may know how much they can take.

At Penton it should be always summer, with dog-roses and sweetbriar, with placid red cows grazing on the tender grass, with boats tethered in the lazy current round the bend of the Hook.

An uncommonly good place for fishing it is, this Hook, as the kingfishers have found out, for they are yearly increasing, and apparently do not mind the gay tide of summer company that invades their haunts. Right down on the banks near the lock one pair nested this year. No steamers churn up the waters and frighten the fish; only a slow-moving house-boat or two towed to position and there left, or those drifting boats belonging to young men and maidens who are content to drift metaphorically as well as actually.

The Abbey river starts away on its own account on the far side of the Hook, and begins its short course of about a couple of miles, to fall into the Thames again at Chertsey. It used to be possible to get up it in a boat, but now it is barred. However, visitors have nothing to complain of, for the meadows around are singularly open to them, and the place is not hedged about with restrictions as are so many river resorts. Numbers of people come down to picnic, and it is no uncommon sight to see quite a row of motors outside the lock-keeper's house, while footman or chauffeur carries across the luncheon hampers to what was once a peninsula but is now an island. Tradesmen's carts come round too, finding in the swallow-colony quite enough demand to make it worth their while; and year by year the bungalows grow. A whole new piece of meadow, hitherto osier bed, is even now going to be devoted to them. "Why, I get as many as twenty to thirty applications for land every week," says the lock-keeper. It is to be hoped Penton

Hook will not become over-populated, or the delightful freedom from conventionality which now characterises it might die away. "Ladies who come down here—why, some of them, they never put a hat on their heads the whole time, and I was going to say not shoes or stockings either!" The place is particularly sought after by theatrical people. Miss Ellen Terry still holds the bungalow she has had for many years. It is surprising how early the season begins; even at the end of chilly March a few of the first of the swallows appear.

CHAPTER XVI

ABOUT CHERTSEY AND WEYBRIDGE

BETWEEN Chertsey and Penton Hook is Laleham, where the tiny ivy-covered church is too much hidden away to be seen easily. An old red brick moss-grown wall is the chief object near the river, and with the bending trees and quiet fields there is a sense of brooding peace which only remains in places off the main roads. Matthew Arnold was born at Laleham and is buried in the churchyard. His father, Dr. Arnold of Rugby, came here in 1819, but he left when Matthew was only six, to take the head-mastership of Rugby.

Between Laleham and Chertsey there is some open, rather untidy ground on which gypsies are wont to camp. It cannot be said that the river looks its best above Chertsey. The country is too flat and open, and on a summer day one is too often scorched. Yet there is always some beauty to be found, and it is certainly in open spaces like these that we see best reflected "heaven's own blue." Away to the west the tiny Abbey river flows in past a mill. By Chertsey bridge a triumphant victory in regard to right-of-way over the Thames Conservancy in 1902, is recorded on two newly built villas. Opposite is the Bridge Hotel, which, with its little bay, its Lombardy poplars and green lawn, is a pleasant oasis.

Chertsey Abbey, which was of great fame, lay between the town and the river. It was founded in 666, and some Saxon tiles from the flooring may be seen in the British Museum. The buildings were destroyed by the Danes, but it was re-established in 964 as a Benedictine Monastery.

Nothing shows more the immense power of the

monks in England than these mighty abbeys which studded the country. We have come across so many, even in our short journey between Oxford and London, that the fact cannot escape notice; though they probably were more thickly set beside the river than elsewhere, because, as I have said, flowing water attracted these old monks for more than one reason. There is hardly anything left of Chertsey Abbey now, yet in its prime it was like a small town, giving employment to hundreds of people. There are a few ivy-covered steps near the back of the church and an old bit of wall doubtfully supposed to have been part of the boundary; this is near the Abbey river. Henry VI. was buried at Chertsey, and his funeral is referred to in Shakespeare's play of *Richard III.:*

> . . after I have solemnly interr'd
> At Chertsey monast'ry this noble king,
> And wet his grave with my repentant tears.

So he makes the hypocritical Duke of Gloucester speak. Cowley, the poet, lived in Chertsey for two years before his death. The house still stands; it has an overhanging storey and is covered with rough stucco. Charles James Fox was born in a house near, and this probably decided him in making choice of a residence many years later, for he chose St. Anne's Hill, only two miles away, which can be seen far and wide around. There he settled to indulge in the delightful hobby of improving his grounds.

Below Chertsey Bridge is an excellent punting reach, where the championship punting competition is held every year in the beginning of August. This is, doubtless, the reason why Chertsey is crowded with visitors in the summer, when out of all the innumerable lodgings scarcely a room is to be had.

The river about Weybridge and Shepperton is much more varied than at Chertsey, and to my mind variety is a direct element of beauty in river scenery. We have passed through flat meadows lined with straight ranks of Lombardy poplars that might belong to northern France, and then suddenly, at Weybridge, we begin once more curves and twists and unexpected islands and snug corners. There is a ferry across the river, and the place seems to get along wonderfully well without a bridge. In the middle of the stream is a well-kept island which belonged to the late Mr. D'Oyly Carte; it is hedged about with an exclusive wall, enclosing a pretty garden. In the centre is a neat white house with projecting tiles.

In every direction there are numerous boat-building establishments. The lock island is large and has other buildings on it besides the lock-keeper's cottage. It is a favourite camping ground in summer, and has rather an untidy appearance. The wide-mouthed Wey flows in beside a couple of other islands, and is itself a very attractive place to explore, winding away through meadows and beneath overhanging trees. It is, however, not free from locks, though of a somewhat simpler kind than those on the Thames. Weybridge is a fresh and pleasant place, rapidly growing in all directions, and in its gorsy common land and masses of pine woods it reminds one of the parts of Surrey about Camberley. On the green stands the column which once presented seven faces to the seven streets in London, called after it Seven Dials. Since then it has risen in life, having been bought and surmounted with a coronet instead of the dial stone; this was in honour of the Duchess of York, who died in 1820. She lived at Oatlands Park and was very popular.

Oatlands Park is the great place of the neighbourhood. It was once a hunting ground of King

Henry VIII., but now belongs to a large residential hotel. Nothing remains of the building, which was used by many of our English monarchs. George IV. entertained here the Emperor of Russia, the King of Prussia, and all the princes and generals who visited England after Waterloo. In 1790 the Duke of York, who is commemorated by the column in Waterloo Place, bought and rebuilt the house, and still later it was in the possession of the Earl of Ellesmere. Remodelled, the house still stands as the hotel. A large piece of ornamental water in the grounds is almost as great an attraction as Virginia Water. Just where the park touches the river is the place known as Cowey Stakes. It is said that here Cæsar crossed the river when in pursuit of Cassivelaunus, in 54 B.C. The stakes, which are no longer to be seen, are supposed to have been placed there to obstruct his use of the ford. They had been so long under water, that when found they were like ebony; they were about six feet long and shod with iron. They appear to have been too imposing and carefully formed to have been put in for the mere purpose of a river weir or for fishing; but, on the other hand, instead of running with the axis of the river,

WALTON BRIDGE

as would appear reasonable if they were meant to obstruct the passage of men, they were planted across it like a weir. They have afforded matter for endless discussion among antiquaries.

What we know is that Cæsar, having landed at Pevensey, marched inland and came to the Thames at about eighty miles from the sea. The river was fordable only at one place, and here natives were drawn up to oppose him, and the ford fortified with sharp stakes. So the evidence certainly seems in favour of this place.

Near Cowey Stakes is Walton Bridge, on the far side of which is a large pool connected with the river by a channel; here are constantly to be found punt fishers. Turner painted Walton Bridge, and certainly, in some aspects, the place is worthy of being painted. The present bridge is of brick and iron, but the old one was of oak. Walton, like every other place on the Thames, depends greatly on the weather. On days when the cedars are seen against a vivid blue sky and the songs of a thousand birds are heard, when the meadows are lined with flowers, it is beautiful.

> Now rings the woodland loud and long,
> The distance takes a lovelier hue,
> And drown'd in yonder living blue
> The lark becomes a sightless song.

There are other days when the whole is curiously like a platinotype photograph; when the steel-grey water reflects a white sun, and all the countless twigs of the trees are seen in one feathery mass. All colours seem drawn out of the picture, even the green of the grass is turned to dun. Light is everything in estimating beauty, but it is sometimes difficult to realise quite how much one owes to it. We might quote from Cowley's *Hymn to the Light*:

Thou in the moon's bright chariot proud and gay
    Dost thy bright wood of stars survey,
    And all the year dost with thee bring
Of thousand flow'ry lights thine own nocturnal spring.

When, goddess, thou lift'st up thy waken'd head
    Out of the morning's purple bed,
    Thy quire of birds about thee play,
And all the joyful world salutes the rising day.

In Walton Church is a small brass with, *inter alia*, a man riding on a stag's back. The story goes that this man, John Selwyn, was an under-keeper in Oatlands Park in Queen Elizabeth's time, and that when she was present at the "chace," he leapt from his own horse's back straight on to that of the driven stag, when "he not only kept his seat gracefully in spite of every effort of the affrighted beast, but, drawing his

SUNBURY

sword, with it guided him toward the Queen, and coming near her presence plunged it into his throat, so that the animal fell dead at her feet."

In the vestry is a Scolds' or Gossips' bridle, designed in the old days of witch-hunting and other atrocities to torture poor women.

Admiral Rodney was a native of Walton, and an old and quaintly built house which belonged to the regicide Bradshaw is still in existence.

Below Walton is Sunbury with its long, long weirs, and its little houses spread beside the edge of the water. But with Hampton we reach the Londoner's zone, which is for another chapter. At present Halliford and Shepperton, two little places opposite Oatlands, are far too pretty to be passed by without remark. The Manor House at Shepperton has one of the finest lawns on the river, which is no small thing. Shepperton is a scattered place and lies low; the meadows all around are often flooded for miles and miles, looking like an inland sea. A tiny river called the Exe finds its way into the Thames near Halliford. A glimpse of the quaint church of Shepperton should not be missed. The tower is very lean and narrow; it looks rather as if bricks had run short. It was added later than the rest, which was built in 1614. Tradition says that the previous church was destroyed by a Thames flood, though it stood on piles to raise it from the marshy ground. The old rectory, with its dormer windows and projecting wings, is really built of oak, though it has been faced with tiles which look like brick. It is about four hundred years old, and is one of the most delightful rectory houses imaginable. The list of rectors goes back to before 1330.

CHAPTER XVII

THE LONDONER'S ZONE

As far as Hampton the river may be said to lie within the zone of the Londoner. By means of the District Railway and the London and South Western Railway he can get at any part of it, and trams are yearly stretching out further and further, so that he can go above ground, if he wishes, all the way to Hampton. At Hampton itself, at Richmond and Kew, there are large open spaces once the gardens or parks belonging to kings, but now open as public pleasure grounds, ideal places for the man who has a small family to take with him, and whose holiday is limited to a day. For those who are free from encumbrances, there are always boats to be had in abundance, at a much cheaper rate than one would have to pay for them at, say, Maidenhead ; and the scenery itself, though not so fine as some higher up, is pleasant and attractive. If the day be wet or uncertain there is the palace at Hampton to explore ; and accommodation for eating and drinking is amply supplied by numerous inns and hotels clustering round its gates.

The gateway to the Palace is imposing, with its brick piers and stone heraldic animals, and the long low range of buildings on the left side makes a strip of bright colour.

The older part of the palace was built by Wolsey, but by far the greater part of it, as it now stands, is due to William III. Some parts of the entrance gateway and the great hall are all that remain to speak of Wolsey's inconceivable boldness in attempting to build a palace which should outshine that of a jealous monarch like Henry VIII. Skelton's satire, beginning :

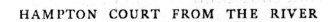

HAMPTON COURT FROM THE RIVER

Why come ye not to courte?
To which courte?
To the kinge's courte,
Or to Hampton Courte?

showed what everyone thought, and doubtless
served to concentrate attention upon Wolsey's
temerity. The irony of the matter lay in the fact
that the palace was not seized, but that the unfortunate owner was forced to make a present of it to
the King:

With turrettes and with toures,
With halls and with boures
Stretching to the starres,
With glass windows and barres;
Hanginge about their walles
Clothes of gold and palles
Fresh as floures in Maye.

Whether he gave the palace as it stood, with its
"two hundred and four score beds, the furniture of
most being of silk," is not recorded; but it is pro-
bable that when he had been wrought up to the
pitch of terror necessary for overcoming his reluc-
tance to part with his beautiful new possession, he
would give all—everything—feeling that so long
as his life was safe it was all he cared about. As a
mark of royal favour, Henry allowed him to occupy
apartments at Richmond, where he was not too
far off to observe the doings of the monarch in

his palace. The king was so pleased with his new establishment that he formed a mighty park, embracing all the land for miles around, including East and West Molesey, Cobham, Esher, Byfleet, and Thames Ditton, and was sorely aggrieved because his loving subjects, whose land and rights had thus been confiscated, dared to make an outcry.

Edward VI. was born at Hampton. After his death Queen Mary came here with her husband Philip, and the unhappy couple, one full of sullen hate, the other sore and bitter in her loneliness, must have strolled in the grounds many a time.

For three months King Charles I. was held prisoner here while his fate was undecided, and when he was removed it was to go up the river to Maidenhead, where he said his last farewell to his children. Oliver Cromwell, who, though he dared not take the name of king, had no dislike to the royal privileges, lived at Hampton, and one of his daughters was married from the palace. But by the time of William III., much of the building had fallen into decay. The situation was pleasant, and though Henry's park had in great part reverted to its rightful owners, there was still much open ground around which made the place desirable. William had a passion for building, and loved the prim Dutch style, as was natural. The maze and the canal, and the long avenues of trees in Bushey, are all evidences of his taste. But in the palace he attempted to copy Versailles, as he had already copied it at Kensington. Poor Wren must have been as much perplexed as ever he was in his life when told to remodel a Tudor building into the copy of one of the Renaissance, and that he succeeded at all is greatly to his credit. Two out of the five courts which remained of the old palace were pulled down, and the state rooms, as we now see them, are the work of Wren under William's directions. Since then the interest and beauty of the interior has been much added to by the famous collection of pictures, which attracts at least as many visitors as the building does.

Bushey Park adjoins Hampton, and lies so close to the river that it forms part of the river scenery. Its glory is in its great double line of chestnuts, with the broad sweep of green grass lining the avenues formed by them. Chestnut Sunday, when the trees are in bloom, is a well-known date in the Londoner's calendar, and every description of conveyance is hired, chartered, or borrowed, to see the great sight. Hundreds of people, to whom it is one of the great days in the year, walk about or

eat refreshments beneath the sombre green masses
which are lightened by a thousand pyramidal
candles. The central avenue is one mile and forty
yards in length, and the width of it is fifty-six
yards. A noble conception, worthy of the little
man with the wise head. On Hampton Green,
outside the gates of the palace, Sir Christopher
Wren passed the last five years of his life, in sight
of his greatest architectural problem.

Molesey Lock, just above the bridge, is a popular
place in summer. All those who have come down
to enjoy the fresh air, and who want an excuse for
doing nothing, stand and watch the boats passing
through; there is always as great a crowd on the
tow-path as on the water. A number of islands
lie above the lock, the largest of which is Tagg's, as
well known as any island on the river, and much
patronised by holiday-makers at lunch and tea
time. In summer a band plays on the lawn twice
a week. It is opposite the end of the Hurst Park
Racecourse, patronised by altogether a different type
of people from those who come to Hampton Court,
and who can only be said to belong to the river
accidentally, by reason of the position of the course.
A wonderful club boat-house of polished wood
has sprung up of recent years on the Hampton

side, and above it is Garrick's Villa with portico and columns. This the great actor bought in 1754, and kept until his death, after which his widow lived in it for another forty years. He was visited here by all the celebrated men of his time, including Horace Walpole, Dr. Johnson and Hogarth, and here he gave a splendid series of river fêtes. The little temple on the bank was built by him as a shrine for a statue of Shakespeare, which has now been removed. A small public garden on the edge of the water makes this a favourite lounging place for the people of the neighbourhood. The scenery is rather tame, but has that charm always to be found in flowing water and green grass, in the absence of chimneys and other horrors of man's making.

The church of Hampton village stands up fairly high above the water. It is in a most unlovely style, but ivy has done something to smooth down its defects, which are further toned by distance. There is a ferry close by, and as this is the nearest point to the station, many of those who arrive by train on race-days cross at this point, and the ferrymen reap rich harvests.

Not far beyond this loom up the great earthworks and reservoirs of the West Middlesex and Grand Junction Water Company, and with that the influence of Hampton may be said to cease.

Returning again to the bridge at Hampton, we
have the river Mole flowing in on the right bank.
Molesey Regatta takes place every year in July.
The trees and red brickwork of the palace are on
the left, and only a short way down is the pretty
little oasis of Thames Ditton, which somehow seems
as if it ought to belong to the river much higher
up, and had fallen here by mistake.   The Swan
Inn is right on the edge of the water.   It is proud
of the fact that Theodore Hook wrote a verse on a
pane of glass at a time when such things were quite
legitimate, because the tourist, as we know him,
had not then come into existence to vulgarise the
practice.   The pane has been broken, but the
verse is remembered, and the following lines are a
sample:

> The Swan, snug inn, good fare affords
>   As table e'er was put on,
> And worthier quite of loftier boards,
>   Its poultry, fish and mutton.
> And while sound wine mine host supplies,
>   With ale of Meux and Tritton,
> Mine hostess with her bright blue eyes
>   Invites to stay at Ditton.

We wonder how many hostesses since have
wished the lines had never been written.   An old
inn near by, with overhanging gable end and

clinging wistaria, makes a pretty corner, and in the High Street itself there are bits so different from the Kingston and Surbiton ideal, that one cannot understand how they can be in the same zone with them at all. The green lawns of Ditton House and Boyle Farm are quite close, and the fine island with its willows hides the flatness of the further bank.

About the end of the eighteenth century this part of the river was celebrated for its magnificent fêtes.

One of these, given at Boyle Farm, inspired Moore to write a poem which was not published until long after:

> Lamps of all hues, from walks and bowers,
> Broke on the eye like kindling flowers
> Till budding into light each tree
> Bore its full fruit of brilliancy.
>
>   *   *   *   *
>
> And now along the waters fly
> Swift gondoles of Venetian breed,
> With knights, and dames, who calm reclined,
> Lisp out love sonnets as they glide,
> Astonishing old Thames to find
> Such doings on his moral tide.

The reach is a favourite one for sailing boats. Below Long Ditton are the large waterworks of the Lambeth Company. On fine Saturdays and

Sundays the Hampton tow-path on the other side is generally alive with people. On Raven's Ait is the club-house of the Kingston Rowing Club, and beside the water runs a well laid out strip of ground with bushes and seats, and a good stout hedge to keep off the dust from the motor cars which race by on the road—a section of the Ripley Road beloved of scorchers. In summer this little public garden is bright with flowers, and it is a great favourite with the inhabitants of Kingston and Surbiton. Before arriving at the bridge there are the backs of untidy houses, and generally a great medley of barges, laden with hay and bricks and coal, lying about by the wharves.

Kingston, as we have said elsewhere, can boast of one of the oldest bridges over the river. A bridge of wood stood here in 1225, when there was no other in the whole sweep downward as far as London Bridge. The present one is very narrow, and its convenience is not increased since a double line of tramways has been laid across it. The general similarity of position between it and Richmond Bridge may be remarked. Both have large boat-building establishments near, and both are about the same distance from the railway bridges which cross below them.

As this is not a guide-book, no attempt is made to describe other than picturesque effects and ancient survivals such as are likely to attract the notice of anyone actually on the river, but an exception must be made in favour of Kingston Stone, which anyone ought to land to see. It is in the market-place, not five minutes from the river, and from it—the King's Stone—the name of the place is derived. It is a shapeless block, mounted on a granite base, and round it are inscribed the names of seven Saxon kings who were crowned here, and a silver penny of each of their reigns has been inserted. There seems to be no authentic history of this interesting relic, and no definite explanation as to why these kings should have been here crowned; but a suggestion there is that at the date of the first of the coronations Mercia and Wessex were joined under one king, and while the boundaries of Mercia reached to the Thames on the north side, those of Wessex marched with them on the south. Kingston was equally accessible to both, and as London was at that time in the hands of the Danes, and the ford at Kingston the only one above London by which the river could be safely crossed, the place was chosen accordingly.

Teddington Lock was for a long time the lowest

on the river, but has been supplanted by a Benjamin in the shape of a half-tide lock at Richmond. The reach about Teddington is in the summer very pretty. The banks are dotted with little bungalows, bright with blue and white paint and gay with flowers. The long smooth lawns of the riverside houses stretch down to the water, and the Crimson Rambler climbs over many a rustic bridge and iron trellis. It is a well-cared for part, and holds its own against rivals of greater grandeur. There are several islands forming cover where one can ship oars and rest, and though landing is in most places forbidden, there is no law against a boat's drawing inshore beneath the shelter of the overhanging trees, amongst which may be noted several weeping willows. This bit recalls Moore's :

> .   .   .   .   where Thames is seen
> Gliding between his banks of green,
> While rival villas on each side
> Peep from their bowers to win his tide.

Beyond Teddington we are in Twickenham Reach :

> Where silver Thames round Twit'nam meads
> His winding current sweetly leads.
> —*Walpole.*

There is a great bend at Twickenham, and in it the chimneys of Strawberry Hill may be seen overtopping the high evergreen hedge that surrounds it.

The house has been altered considerably since Walpole's date, but in its essence it is the house he built. He himself describes his view thus :

> Directly before it is an open grove through which you see a field, which is bounded by a serpentine wood of all kind of trees, and flowering shrubs, and flowers. The lawn before the house is situated on the top of a small hill from whence to the left you see the town and church of Twickenham, encircling a turn of the river, that looks exactly like a seaport in miniature. The opposite shore is a most delicious meadow, bounded by Richmond Hill, which loses itself in the noble woods of the park to the end of the prospect on the right, where is another turn of the river, and the suburbs of Kingston as luckily placed as Kingston is on the left. . . . You must figure that all this is perpetually enlivened by a navigation of boats and barges.

His architecture was a medley of everything that could by any possibility be included under the heading Gothic, and the result was more curious than beautiful, though it became the fashion to visit the house. Walpole bemoaned the crowds aloud, but secretly delighted in them. He published a description of the house, in the beginning of which he says he trusts it will be a lesson in taste to all who see it ! An example of the suave self-belief of an egotist. At Twickenham there is another fantastic building called Pope's Villa. This can be seen much better from the river than Straw-

berry Hill can, and it is an affected piece of architecture.   It has been described as "a combination
of an Elizabethan half-timber house and a Stuart
Renaissance, with the addition of Dutch and Swiss,
Italian and Chinese features."   This is not the
house occupied by Pope, nor is it even exactly on
the same site as his.   In front of it is a group of
weeping willows, a kind of tree which shows to
particular advantage by the water-side.   Pope
himself is said to have been the first to introduce
it into England, having found some sticks of it
in a bundle sent to him from Spain by the Countess
of Suffolk.

Pope lived at Twickenham from 1719 to
1744, and produced here most of his important
works, including the last books of his *Odyssey*,
the *Dunciad* and the famous *Essay on Man*.
He was here visited by Gay and Swift, and
many another contemporary whose name is still
held in estimation.   He laid out his grounds in
a decorative way, and made a curious underground grotto, which lies away from the water,
on the other side of the road.   Among the
celebrated men who have, at one time or
another, lived at Twickenham are numbered
Henry Fielding, Dr. Donne, Sir Godfrey Kneller,

Tennyson, and Turner. The last-named was very fond of fishing, and used to fish a good deal in this part of the river.

There is a little esplanade at Twickenham, shaded by small horse-chestnuts, and in front lies the famous Eel-pie Island, which vies with Tagg's in summer popularity. The hotel has a pleasant garden, but the rest of the island is, it must be confessed, rather untidy, with several places for building motor launches and many boat-houses. At the small wharf opposite the church there are nearly always barges unloading bricks or sand and gravel. Yet the place has an air of dignity, perhaps given to it by the old Perpendicular stone tower of the church, so incongruously welded on to a red-brick pedimented Georgian building. The architect was the same who built St. George's, Hanover Square; but, as Sir Godfrey Kneller was church-warden, one might have expected something in better taste. Pope is buried inside, and a flat slab with his initial letter on it now serves as a base for several pews. Not far from the church is York House, and with Orleans and Ham House on the other side of the river this is a notable group. In the great gardens of Orleans House grow splendid cedars, stone pines, and other evergreens. The little Duke of Gloucester, the only child who survived babyhood out of Queen Anne's enormous family, was brought here for his health in 1694. Six years later this quaint child, with a rickety body and an enormous head, died of small-pox at the age of eleven. The house was afterwards rebuilt. To it in 1800 came Louis Philippe, then Duc d'Orleans, and his two brothers. After his brief summer of prosperity in France, he returned to England as an exile in 1848; that he had a warm remembrance of the house is shown by his then purchasing it. He did not, however, live here himself, but placed his son, the Duc d'Aumale, in it, and a colony of royal refugees settled round. At Mount Lebanon, not far off, was the Prince de Joinville; and the Duc d'Aumale, having bought York House, gave it to his nephew the Comte de Paris, who lived there for six or seven years. Queen Anne was born in York House—it had been given to her mother's father, Lord Clarendon—and with her elder sister she spent her earliest years at Twickenham. All these notable houses and dignified memories are enough to account for the air of sober gravity never wholly absent from the river at Twickenham even on the brightest days; and the rows of Lombardy poplars, the magnificent cedars,

and the fine foliage of the other trees enhance the impression. Ham House, on the other side, was built in 1611, it is said for Prince Henry, James I.'s eldest son. It is screened from the water by a row of tall trees. Around it grow Scotch firs and holm oaks.

We have not long left Twickenham before we see the little oblong island about which there was so much contention because it formed an item in the famous Marble Hill view, seen from the heights of Richmond Park. The London County Council are now owners of the Marble Hill estate, and have made it into a public park. It lies on the Twickenham side. The house was built by George II. for the Countess of Suffolk. Gay, Pope, and Swift all took an interest in the building, and voiced their opinions as to the style and the laying out of the grounds. A suite of rooms in the house was afterwards set aside for Gay, who was a great favourite with the countess.

The other side of the river is open, and it must be admitted that on a sunny day this bit is a stiff pull if one is unfortunate enough to be going against the current. It is often to be described by the word "glaring," yet the fine scimitar-like sweep of the tree-crowned heights above, capped by the huge mass of the Star and Garter Hotel, toned to unoffending mediocrity of colour, is worth seeing.

Richmond, like nearly all the other places on the river, has an atmosphere of its own, difficult to put into words. It is less flippant than Kingston, and has not a tinge of the gravity of Twickenham. The houses rise high and are irregular; those in the main street recede from the water as they leave the bridge, and between them and the stream are innumerable others, some with gardens, some overshadowed by trees. Weeping willows, Scotch firs, and ivy-covered trunks abound, and the place is the perfection of a residential quarter. There is enough oldness and irregularity to avoid stiffness, enough modernity to ensure cleanliness. The bridge has a peculiarly individual curve—a real humpback—and its stone balustrade is very fine. At the southern end, far too many new red-brick flats are springing up, alas! but on the north or east, where lies old Richmond, they are not visible to any appreciable extent. The scene below the bridge is distinctly pretty. Large boat-building yards, as at Kingston, occupy the foreground, and the warm cinnamons and ochres of newly-varnished boats are generally to be seen, as well as the more crude and garishly painted craft. The islands are tree-covered, and are well placed in the stream. Yet one may note that, popular as Richmond is, it is not flooded in the summer time with such crowds of boating visitors as Hampton. There are more large craft about, and boating people do not care for that.

What remains of Richmond Palace must be sought below the bridge, for it will not be seen without a little effort. The old palace stood right on the margin of the water, and an engraving of it is still extant, showing a pinnacled and many chimneyed building. The angular towers are capped by turrets like those of the old palace at Greenwich. Henry I. was the first English king to live here, but until Edward III.'s time it was hardly a recognised royal palace. It fell before the hand of Richard II., who in a fit of frenzy at the death of his wife, which occurred here, ordered its destruction. Henry V. restored it, but it was burnt down in the end of the fifteenth century, and afterwards rebuilt by Henry VII., who changed its name from Sheen to Richmond, and who himself died there. The old Tudor gateway of his time remains still. It is said, but with doubtful accuracy, that the Countess of Nottingham died in the room over the gateway, after having confessed to Elizabeth her duplicity about the Earl of Essex and the ring he had confided to her charge. We have many records of Richmond from the time of the miserable Katherine of Arragon—widow of one boy prince, but not yet affianced to the other, a foreigner in a strange land, bitterly hating her surroundings—to the time of Charles I., who made the great park and hunted in it. A large Carthusian monastery stood near the palace. Perkin Warbeck found an asylum in the monastery, and in 1550 Robert Dudley was here married to Amy Robsart.

There is a half-tide lock at Richmond, with a footbridge. This is at present the lowest lock on the river, though there is some talk of making a similar one at Wandsworth. It is quite different in construction from the usual kind. It has three great sluices, each weighing thirty-two tons, and when the tide brings up the water, so that it is equal with that above—that is to say, at half-tide— the sluices are raised by the addition of a small weight to the massive pendules by which they are exactly balanced, and the water is allowed free way.

All along this stretch of the river there is on one side a fine row of shady trees growing to a great height. Beyond the raised footpath is the old Deer Forest, on which stands Kew Observatory, and a minor stream, which afterwards forms a moat to Kew Gardens, runs along merrily. Isleworth is finely placed at a bend of the river, and though it is a manufacturing place, it is not so bad as Brentford. The large willow-covered ait in front affords occupation to the osier gatherers. The church is ugly; it is placed very like that at Hampton, and, like Hampton also, its ugliness is mitigated by a covering of ivy. The tower, as so frequently happens, is much older than the rest. Was it that church towers were built more solidly than the naves, or that the naves would have stood equally well had they been allowed to remain?

Then we come to the great park surrounding Syon House (Duke of Northumberland), a park fringed with marshy ground, where reeds and rushes flourish, and which is overflowed at every flood. Crows consider it a delightful place, if their perpetual presence may be taken to indicate opinion. A great clump of cedars stands between the house and the river, but we have to go considerably further on before the severe line of frontage, with its ground floor arcade and battlemented parapet, can be seen at full length. The astonished lion stands clear up against the sky, as he did of old at Northumberland House, over the site of which now flows a ceaseless stream of traffic. Long years ago there stood here at Isleworth a convent for nuns. This was suppressed at the Dissolution. Katherine Howard was imprisoned in Syon House until three days before her execution, and only five years later the corpse of her murderer, the tyrant Henry, stopped here on its way to Windsor. Edward VI. granted the place to Lord-Protector Somerset, who, with his usual mania for building, began to reconstruct it on a much larger scale; but before he had got farther than the mere shell of his design, he suffered disgrace, and Syon House passed to the Duke of Northumberland. Here came Lady Jane Grey, timid and doubting, to receive the offer of the crown, and from here she started on her last sad journey to the Tower.

Queen Mary naturally tried to re-establish the nuns, but found it difficult, as some had died and others had married! Fuller's comment is worth quoting:

> It was some difficulty to stock it with such as had been veiled before, it being now thirty years since the Dissolution, in which time most of the elder nuns were in their graves, and the younger in the arms of their husbands, as afterwards embracing a married life.

In James I.'s reign Syon House was in the hands of the Earl of Northumberland, who also fell under his sovereign's displeasure, but was allowed to return here to die. Under his successor, the tenth earl, Inigo Jones was employed to alter the house; but the architect of the present building was Adam (1728-92).

The place is often very quiet, and the hovering crows, and perhaps a few men in boats grubbing for sand and gravel from the river-bed with long-handled scoops, have it all to themselves. It is not much frequented because just below comes Brentford, with all its ugliness, a sore blot on the river. Nevertheless, on the Surrey side, to counterbalance it, we have the famous Kew Gardens. The very varied trees that grow here can be well seen, for the parapet of the wall is low, the Gardens being sufficiently protected by the moat. Further on, when this comes to an end, the wall is heightened, and only the tops of the elms and ashes and horse-chestnuts peep over. Presently a new object comes into view—a "palace," in that it was the dwelling-place of royalty; but anything less like a palace surely never was seen. A stiff, square red-brick house, where Miss Burney served her "sweet queen," and the old king cried "What, what, what?" a hundred times a day, and the overflowing quiverful of their Royal Highnesses quarrelled and played and grew up.

Very few people realise what a large basin there is on the river Brent, and what an amount of business is carried on here. From the river, one's chief reflection is thankfulness that the trees on the large islands have grown so well that they form a screen for the soap factories, the cement works, the breweries, etc., which constitute the industries of Brentford.

> Brentford, tedious town,
> For dirty streets and white-legged chickens known,

says Gay. The dirty streets are still there, with the confusion in their narrow limits worse confounded by the passing of tramcars, which, over the mile along which Brentford spreads itself, take double the time spent on any other bit of equal distance on their route. Most people have a hazy notion about two kings at Brentford; this is one of those curious examples of the persistence of an unimportant detail. The allusion was first made in a play called *The Rehearsal*, written by the Duke of Buckingham, and Thackeray's ballad on the same subject carried it a step further. That there was a battle at Brentford one learns in the history books. It was when the Parliamentarians, who had rested in the town all night, were surprised by Prince Rupert, under the cover of a thick mist, and completely routed.

All along the Kew side, up to the bridge, are tea-gardens sandwiched between boat-houses; and the new bridge made of granite, with its branching lamps and royal arms, is really an imposing object. Above and below the bridge the character of the river is singularly different. Above, as we have seen, are the mudflats, and wharves, and chimneys, not to omit water towers and gasometers; and below is a bit of Chiswick, built along by the waterside, a queer little irregular row of red-brick houses and cottages, near which are fastened the boats of men who live by fishing; it is a little riverside place of the old sort. There are meadows, called Duke's Meadows, opposite Mortlake; these afford a fine vantage-ground for spectators who come to see the great Boat Race.

The hour of the Boat Race varies according to the tide, for the race is rowed at the " top of the tide "—when it is at its fullest. If the hour be an easy one—about mid-day—and the weather is promising, and especially if the reports of the prowess of the crews give reason to believe the race will be a close one, then the crowd is very large indeed. Some prefer to watch the start; some enthusiasts keep up with the boats on water the whole way; but a great majority there are who want to see the last effort between Hammersmith and Barnes Bridges, for it is almost a certainty that the crew leading at Barnes Bridge will be the winner. Almost, but not quite; for there was an occasion when, by a sudden spurt, the positions of the boats were reversed, and Cambridge, which had been behind, won the race. The road along by Mortlake is lined with crowds; every window is filled, and all available roofs. On the railway bridge are closely-packed ranks of people, brought there and deposited by trains, which afterwards decorously withdraw and wait to pick them up again. The price of this first-rate position is included in the fares. Chiswick meadows afford space for many more persons, who usually pay a shilling a head to the land-holders. This is a very favourite position, because the grassy slopes form such a pleasant seat while the inevitable waiting is gone through.

In the river itself lie several steamers packed with passengers, and also various small boats.

Then down comes the launch of the Thames Conservators to clear the course. The long strings of barges, which have been taking advantage of the flowing tide to make their way up-stream, are seen no more. A gun goes off, and then, an extraordinarily short time after, a murmur begins among the crowds on the Mortlake side. It grows and grows and swells along the Chiswick shore, as first one boat creeps round the corner, and then the other. "Cambridge wins; Cambridge, Cambridge!" "Row up, Oxford!"

Then, perhaps—usually—it is seen that one boat is leading by so many lengths as to make it impossible for the other to catch up. The leading boat goes ahead with a straight, splendid swing into clear water. The losing one, getting into its opponent's wash, rocks as it labours on, its crew lose heart, and the distance widens.

Close behind are the umpire's launch and a dozen others gliding along, keeping just behind the backward crew. And when all have passed, the river, so calm before, is churned up into miniature waves that wash and beat on the banks. Presently the umpire's boat is seen coming swiftly back, bearing the winning flag at the bows over the other.

The trains move slowly forward to pick up the passengers ; bicycles, motors, and carriages begin to move off ; streams of people pour down every road ; and all is over for another year.

The chief memory of Chiswick is that of Hogarth, who is buried in the churchyard close by the water. The house in which he lived is still standing, and is a few minutes' walk from the church. Hogarth was here for about three years, though when he left to go to Leicester Square he did not sell the house, and his widow lived in it after his death. For two years Pope also lived in Chiswick ; and in Chiswick House, which lies away from the river on the other side of the fields, two great men, Charles James Fox and George Canning, died in the same room, in 1806 and 1827 respectively. And in the Roman Catholic Cemetery at Mortlake is the massive sarcophagus—in the form of an Arab tent—beneath which lies the dust of the great traveller, Sir Richard Burton, and his wife.

CHAPTER XVIII

THE RIVER AT LONDON

THERE is a subtle difference in the river above and below Hammersmith: above, it is a stream of pleasure —below, it is something less beautiful, but grander, more crowded with memories, more important.

Though pleasure boats are to be seen in quantities any summer evening about Putney; though market gardens still border the banks at Fulham; yet the river is for the greater part lined with wharves and piers and embankments.   It is no wild thing running loose, but a strong worker full of earnest purpose.   It is the great river without which there would have been no London, the river which bears the largest trade the world has ever known.

Unfortunately, the habit of using the river at London as a highway was lost some time in the eighteenth century and has not yet been recovered, notwithstanding the gallant attempt of the London County Council to educate the people to it.   At one time the river was used for every sort of traffic: tilt boats, covered with an awning, ran up and down like omnibuses and charged sixpence a passenger; and every man of importance kept his private barge, for the smoothly gliding waters made an infinitely preferable route to the vile roads.   At every set of stairs—and the stairs were frequent—numberless wherries awaited hire. In the sixteenth century there were two thousand on the water, and it was reckoned that nine thousand watermen earned their living by transporting people up and down or from shore to shore.   When it is objected that these men were a pest and a nuisance, so that we are well rid of them, that their language was unspeakable and their

BEYOND HAMMERSMITH BRIDGE

manners filthy, it may be replied, *autres temps autres mœurs*, for there are a few watermen still to be had at Westminster, at the Tower, and at most of the river stairs, and they are civil and obliging, only, alas, the public rarely patronises them. Occasionally, an uncommonly adventurous person, probably a visitor staying in London, penetrates to the haunt of the watermen, and, upon inquiry, he finds a respectable man, duly licensed like a cabman, liable to be reported for rudeness or misconduct, strictly limited by law as to the fees he may demand, and ready to add greatly to the pleasure of the trip by his genial, shrewd humour and his keen observation; qualities found frequently in men whose business is upon great waters.

Without counting the railways, fourteen bridges now span the Thames from Hammersmith downward, and even fourteen we sometimes find inadequate to our needs in this hurrying life. Not until the middle of the eighteenth century was the historic London Bridge backed up by a second. Before that time, all men crossed by boat, or by the ferry at Westminster, or even by the ford there, a feat which the embanking of the river has long rendered impossible.

We can see it, this great river of ours, as in
a vision, gradually emerging from its primeval
wilderness. First it spread widely between the
rising ground on each side, a vast area of lagoons,
flooded at high tide, and at low tide a swampy
place full of half-submerged islets. Then one or
two small settlements for trade were planted on
its banks, first at Westminster, and others about
the site of Cannon Street Station, where the
Walbrook leapt to meet the larger current. There
was a gradual extension of houses along the
brink. At last an attempt was made to bridge
the river over, probably by a wooden bridge.
This succeeded, and when the bridge had stood
for some time it was replaced by another in
the twelfth century. This was built and rebuilt,
as the turbulent river, feeling the erection of
earthworks to curtail its flood, fretted to be free,
and rushed seaward with force, tearing down the
obstruction offered by this quaint old London
Bridge with its double line of houses. Many a
picture of this bridge still remains. It was a
fascinating, a wonderful structure. Numberless
children have yearned to have lived there, high
above the flood. What delight to look out from
one's nursery window and see the grey-green

THE CUSTOM HOUSE

water hastening past. To see it mysteriously stop as if by some command from on High, then slowly turn and race inward again. Marvellous feat! Miraculous bridge! There was a beautiful chapel, a veritable gem of work, upon this bridge. There was a house like a puzzle-house, put together with pegs, without an iron nail in it. There were gateways at each end, and on the gateways were the grisly remains of the heads of men and women who had been executed. There were shops on each side of the road where ribbons and laces and other haberdashery might be bought at will.

There were gaps between the houses, where one could escape for a moment from the lumbering, creaking, groaning traffic pent up in the narrow, mud-splashed roadway, and see the water itself, and see how the houses were built out over it, resting on nothing. Another miracle! A mighty tome might be written about Old London Bridge; of all the relics of a past London, it is the one I should like most to have seen. Mills there were on this bridge, to which the people could bring their corn to be ground by the force of the water. Waterworks there were, too, and the bridge itself contained a drawbridge to protect London against invasion, for, as there was none other crossing, an enemy prevented here might well be held in check altogether.

Next to London Bridge, the oldest bridge across the river was at Kingston, and it is on record that in 1554, Sir Thomas Wyatt, finding London Bridge closed against him, marched all the way to Kingston in order to cross, but on arrival there, found that he had been anticipated, and that the bridge was broken down.

The present London Bridge has been recently widened. At one end of it rises the white tower of St. Magnus, a Danish saint, and behind it is the pointing finger of the Monument, while down the river are the market of Billingsgate, the quay of the Custom House, and beyond, rising tall and ghostly, close to the Tower itself, the Tower Bridge, the latest addition to the list.

On the south side of London Bridge, over the houses peep the pinnacles of St. Saviour's tower, Southwark. Anciently, it was called St. Mary Overies, and was once a priory, one of the most ancient houses in London. From this there ran a ferry, which was in use long after the bridge was built, for the narrowness of the street and the continual blocks made a passage by the bridge a

DUTCH BARGES NEAR THE TOWER

process of time.   Gower, the poet, was a benefactor
to the priory, and is buried in the church.

As the Tower Bridge can swing open, ships of
all sizes can get up as far as London Bridge, when
the tide allows them sufficient water-way, and
a busy scene, watched by a never-failing crowd of
idlers, is always to be witnessed in the reach
below.   Ships there are of all shapes and sizes,
but mostly hideous, made for merchandise and
not for show.   Many of them are iron, and
run between eight and twelve hundred tons.
They come from Hamburg, Hull, Newcastle,
Holland, and many another port.   There, out in
the river, is a dredger working with a hideous grind-
ing noise, and beyond it are two or three brilliantly
painted green and red boats with great wooden
flaps, or lee boards, on their sides.   They are
Dutch eel boats, and are allowed to lie in the river
free from dues, if they keep always in the same
place.   It is a survival of an ancient custom.

As we pass through under London Bridge, and
come out on the other side, we can see the grey
river with its bustling craft, framed like a series
of pictures in the wide arches.

Some of the oldest theatres in London stood
on the part called Bankside, about Southwark

Bridge; at present the view is dingy and uninteresting. The Bishop of Winchester's palace once adjoined Bankside, as that of the Archbishop of Canterbury, at Lambeth, still stands near Westminster Bridge; but it fell into ruins and the bishops removed to Chelsea.

It is impossible to enumerate the palaces and fine houses that once stood along Thames Street, which, in the fourteenth century, was the most fashionable street in London. The part of the foreshore now occupied by wharves and great warehouses—where cranes swing and lighters await their loads all day long, and every working day— has all been reclaimed from the river. Once it was covered at every returning tide, but strong piles were driven into the mud, and on this unpromising spot houses began to rise and débris accumulated, until firm ground was made, and this became one side of a busy street.

On the up-side of Cannon Street, close to the cavernous jaws of the station, is a wharf marked in white letters, "Walbrook Wharf." This is as near as we can get to the first site of London, where the Briton made his modest lake-fort, Llyn-din, and afterwards the Romans pitched their strong citadel.

THE TOWER OF ST. MAGNUS

Queenhithe was given by King John to his mother, Queen Eleanor. Hence arose the name. It was no trifling gift, for this was the most important dock on the Thames at that time, and dues were collected from all the ships unlading here. Now it is a small area in which the water laps at rotting lichened posts as it slowly uncovers and re-covers the slimy mud.

The whole of this district lying north of the Thames is the oldest part of our ancient city, and it is thick with memories. Down the crooked streets Spenser came as a boy from his home beyond the city ditch to his school of the Merchant Taylors in Dowgate. Here a fair-haired gentle lad, called Chaucer, loitered many a time, for his father's house was in Thames Street.

Not far from Puddle dock stood Baynard's Castle with its high buttressed walls. In it Edward IV. was proclaimed, and in it, also, Richard III. made a feint of refusing the crown belonging to his imprisoned nephew. Tower Royal, Montfichet, and many another glorious building, have gone utterly, so that their sites can be fixed only approximately. The river Fleet, up which large ships could ply once, flowed into the Thames where is now Blackfriars Bridge. By

23

its banks the great religious houses of the Black
and White Friars rose, and the boundary cliff
hewed by its current may still be traced in the
steep rise up Ludgate Hill, which tries the patient
omnibus horses day by day. Over all, as we
draw further up the river, towers the great dome
of St. Paul's.

The Surrey side of the Thames continues
unlovely—a medley of browns and greys, tall
chimneys and tumble-down sheds; it needs the
veil which the atmosphere of London mercifully
throws over it.

The railway bridge and Blackfriars are so close
together, they almost touch. As we pass under-
neath there is a hollow reverberation, like the
beat of the surf in a cave on the shore. Just
above the bridge is anchored the *Buzzard*, the
Naval Volunteer training ship.

Along the northern side now begins the
Embankment, with its solid granite walls and
fringe of young planes. The green lawns and
red buildings of the Temple can be seen only
when the river is very high. Further on is
Somerset House, followed by a line of hotels,
the palaces of modern days. Somerset House is
the successor of the palace built by the arrogant

ST. PAUL'S

Protector Somerset, from the stones of churches and religious buildings ; between it and the Temple stood Arundel and Essex Houses. The latter had earlier been called Leicester House, and Spenser lived there for a time as secretary to the Earl of Leicester.

The tide has turned and is coming in. Little steam tugs, gallantly towing six barges, two abreast and each twice as large as themselves, pant up stream ; while the bargees, with faces the colour of brickdust, the colour they are so fond of reproducing in their paint and even in their sails, stand by their huge rudders. Some barges are struggling along without mechanical aid. The men in charge bend back horizontally in their manipulation of the huge sweeps. There must be a knack in it. No one could work so hard as they seem to be doing ; spine and sinews would give way altogether. Their whole strength results in but a slow progress, and the barge, responding to the push of the water, makes a kind of crab-like movement, sidling up the river broadside on. One, laden with yellow straw till it appears like a huge barn, is stranded right in mid-stream. The long ends of the straw sweep in the water, and there is no moving until the current increases.

Here and there red-brown sails, patched and stained, spring up, and others still furled, stand up along the wharves like crooked warning fingers. Just before Waterloo Bridge there is, neatly tucked away below the Embankment, so that few ever know of its existence, a station of the river police, with trim muslin curtains over the windows.

Between Waterloo and Charing Cross Bridges the same sort of thing continues. An enormous chimney on the Surrey side mocks the dignity of Cleopatra's Needle, now safe in haven after many vicissitudes. The sweep of the river makes these two bridges radiate out like the spokes of a wheel, so that the southern ends are nearer than the northern. The chimneys and wharves and the ubiquitous barges still continue, and as we pass beneath the hideous red iron bridge of Charing Cross, we get a vision of the many towers and pinnacles of Westminster ahead.

Besides the great houses of old times already mentioned, there were others down this stretch of the river too—the Savoy, home of John of Gaunt, and in its time prison and hospital; Durham, Worcester, and Salisbury Houses. These were all either flush with the water or hemmed

THE HOUSES OF PARLIAMENT

in by high walls in which were stairs "to take water at." The only relic of these mansions lies in the watergate of York House, now about a hundred yards from the river, behind a strip of land which has all been reclaimed by the making of the Embankment. But that the Embankment does not always suffice to curb the current was proved not so long ago, for in March, 1906, there was a combination of circumstances which swelled the volume of water abnormally. Sudden floods of rain caused every weir far up the river to be opened, and bounding, exulting to be free, the huge mass of water, swelled by every brook and tributary and swollen to twice its usual size, rushed seaward. But it was met by a high spring tide, and the collision was increased by a strong wind, so that the water rose higher and higher, and the curious spectacle was witnessed of barges floating above the road-way, propelled by sweeps braced against the granite walls. The water burst up through the pavement and the manholes, and ran in a flood under Charing Cross Bridge, but it just did not overtop the Embankment wall by an inch or two, and as the tide subsided the tension relaxed. In the higher reaches, about Barnes and Chiswick, "tide-boards" were used to fill up the crevices below the doors, and by this means alone many a house was saved from being swamped.

The scene is lively enough. Seagulls of all ages—big dingy drab ones and neat ones in liveries of dove-grey and white—float merrily on the ripples, or poise and wheel in the air. Here a County Council steamer ploughs past, churning the river into wavelets, there a lad paddles a boat from shore to shore with a single oar used rudderwise, a feat possible only to a born waterman.

As we pass on we can see the high bastion towers of Scotland Yard. Northumberland Avenue stretches over ground which was once the gardens of Northumberland House—they came down to the water—and beyond this were quadrangles and a medley of buildings, mostly low and mostly of brick, which formed the palace of Whitehall, snatched by Henry VIII. from Wolsey because the royal palace at Westminster had fallen into decay. The Houses of Parliament, standing on the site of the latter palace, are the finest work of Barry, who has been abused for many things, but who seems to have been touched by a genuine spirit of architecture in

WESTMINSTER BY NIGHT

this instance, and to have realised the right characteristics of majesty and delicacy in his work. But he had a noble chance, for the position of the building, standing on the edge of the water, with the bridge rising beside it, gave room for a fine conception.

From Westminster to the Tower or Fleet prison, how many prisoners have come and gone—come up against the current full of hope, and returned of hope bereft! The ghosts are endless, because the river was the usual mode of communication between the Tower and the Court at Westminster, as the Strand was full of holes and seamed by watercourses. If this reach of water were to tell its tale, much of the history of England would be interwoven with it, and it would be tinged with the bitterest sorrow human life can know—death with disgrace.

From the time of Edward the Confessor to the time of Henry VIII., our kings were housed at Westminster as one of the chief of their royal palaces. Luckily the Great Hall, which Rufus built, escaped the fire of 1834, and still may be seen, but all else, with the exception of the crypt of St. Stephen's, has vanished utterly.

The time to see the Houses of Parliament

is undoubtedly at night, when Big Ben's illuminated face sheds a sort of ethereal light on the architectural fretwork near him.

Wordsworth admired the view most in the early morning, before the first waking of the great world of bustle and business:

> The beauty of the morning; silent, bare,
> Ships, towers, domes, theatres and temples lie
> Open unto the fields and to the sky,
> All bright and glittering in the smokeless air.
> Never did sun more beautifully steep
> In his first splendour, valley rock or hill;
> Ne'er saw I, never felt, a calm so deep;
> The river glideth at his own sweet will.
> Dear God, the very houses seem asleep;
> And all that mighty heart is lying still.

Westminster Bridge is particularly wide, and has a low parapet. In the sudden gusts of wind that come sweeping down the river it is a marvel that no one has been caught up and tossed over into the rolling green torrent. These peculiarities also are noticeable when the bridge is seen from the Embankment, for the traffic looms up very high on it, and the omnibuses and cabs look almost as if they were careering along on the parapet itself.

From Westminster to Lambeth is but a short way, and what Westminster Palace was, while it existed, to the lord temporal, so Lambeth has been, and is, to the lord spiritual; from the very earliest times the Archbishops of Canterbury have lodged here.

In our peaceful days the holder of the highest dignity of the Church has not to fear the Tower and the "sharp medicine of the axe" as some of his predecessors did. Laud and Juxon were executed, and for Cranmer there was the worse horror of the torturing stake. Lambeth has seen much cruelty mingled with the name of religion in the time that it has stood above the flood. The Lollards, imprisoned within the tower which still bears their name, made deep incisions on the walls to wile away the weary hours of suspense, and the groans of prisoners have been stifled by these walls as well as by those of the grim Tower.

On the same side as Lambeth, nearer Westminster Bridge, are the curious detached buildings of St. Thomas's Hospital, looking like nothing in the world less than a hospital.

Where Lambeth Bridge is now, was once the ferry by which King James II. passed when he made a hurried exit from the kingdom that repudiated him. It was a bitter night, and, attended by only one gentleman, the king slipped secretly

24

out of his palace at Whitehall, and crossing the
Privy Gardens, made his way to the ferry, where
he entered a small boat with a single pair of oars.
In mid-stream he threw the Great Seal into the
water. A curious and dramatic incident this, that
might well be made the subject of a picture by
some historical painter. The Great Seal was afterwards accidentally drawn up in the net of some
fisherman. But there is another memory further
back still, which gives to this strip of river an
importance which no other part can boast. Here
lay the first ford, to which all the traffic of the
north, on its way to the south coast, had to come.
In the ages before even the oldest London Bridge
was built, a string of pack horses, of weary men
and of travellers, continually wandered down through
the marshes lying around Thorney Island, on which
stands the present Abbey, and, guided by stakes
placed for the purpose, arrived at the river's bank,
there to await low tide, when they could cross over
to the further shore. Through the ages we see
them continuing, and when England was Christian-
ised, to the procession were added monks and
pilgrims bent on holy missions. When London
Bridge was built, a great majority of the age-long
procession was diverted that way, but many still

HAY BARGES NEAR WESTMINSTER BRIDGE

continued to prefer the ancient ford at Westminster. Of course, since the Embankment was made, and the river no longer wanders uncurbed over the lowlands and meadows of Westminster, the current runs deep and strong and no fording is possible.

Above Lambeth we pass the Tate Gallery and the new bridge at Vauxhall, and then traverse a dreary strip of river, dreary on both sides, until we come near to Chelsea Bridge. This is a high-swinging and imposing bridge of the same type as the Albert Bridge further up. How different the Chelsea we see now from the ancient Chelsea. Ours is a Chelsea mainly of red brick, with many tall flats and many beautifully designed houses in pseudo-ancient style. A long line of planes runs along the embankment, which is one of the prettiest embankments on the river. The gardens and green lawns of the Royal Hospital reach to the roadway, and away behind them at some distance can be seen the comparatively low and long range of buildings dating from the time of the Stuarts, and forming an asylum for old soldiers. On the strip of ground to the east of them once stood Ranelagh, the gay rotunda which played such a part in all London flirtations; where misses met their beaux and walked round in stately steps to the sound of music. The breakfasts at Ranelagh were at one time almost as popular as the evening entertainments :

> A thousand feet rustled on mats,
> 　　A carpet that had once been green ;
> Men bowed with their outlandish hats,
> 　　With corners so fearfully keen ;
> Fair maids, who at home in their haste
> 　　Had left all clothing else but a train,
> Swept the floor clean as slowly they paced,
> 　　And then walked round and swept it again.

Thus Bloomfield satirically described the scene. Ranelagh plays a large part in *Evelina* and other romances of that date. The last public entertainment was given in 1803, and of the gay rotunda with its gorgeous fittings not a vestige now remains.

High red-brick flats which stand at the foot of the Royal Hospital gardens by the river, are succeeded by smaller houses, and beyond the Albert Bridge the district has not yet been transformed, as it assuredly will be.

In the small public gardens that face the river there is a bronze statue of Carlyle, the Sage of Chelsea, and not far off rises the curious little tower of dark brick that belongs to the old church, a very mausoleum of tombs. Chelsea has, perhaps, been more altered by the formation of the Embankment than any other part of the river. Its very name implies a bank of shingly beach stretching down to the water, and so it was in old times, and to this beach the gardens of the stately palaces reached. Chelsea has been called a village of palaces. A village it was in old times, quite detached from London, and considered a country residence by many a famous nobleman and statesman. On the site of the row of houses in Cheyne Walk stood the New Manor House built by Henry VIII. as part of the jointure of Catherine Parr, who afterwards lived here with her fourth husband, Thomas Seymour, Lord High Admiral. Both Princess Elizabeth and Lady Jane Grey spent part of their childhood in it. The palace of the Bishops of Winchester, at Southwark, having become dilapidated, as we have seen, a new one was built at Chelsea in 1663, and was occupied by eight successive bishops. Shrewsbury House was another palace built in the reign of Henry VIII. The wife of the Earl of Shrewsbury was the founder of Chatsworth, Oldcotes and Hardwick. In Lawrence or Monmouth House, near the church, lived Smollett the novelist, and further on, somewhere near the end of Beaufort Street, was the house once occupied by Sir Thomas More, whose memory

is still cherished in Chelsea.   No garden among all
the famous gardens of Chelsea was so carefully
tended as his.   When More had been made Lord
Chancellor, and had spent his days hearing cases in
the stuffy precincts of the court, how joyfully must
he have stepped into his barge in the cool of the
evening, to be rowed back up-stream to his roses
and his children, where he could indulge his kindly
humour and his playfulness, and unbend without
fear.   Sometimes the royal barge would sweep up
after him, and the tyrant Harry himself spring
ashore and walk up and down the sweet-scented
alleys, with his arm round the Chancellor's neck, a
dangerous fondness that in time resulted in More's
being cut off altogether from his garden and his
peaceful evenings, and in his going down that
stream never to return.   His monument is in the
church, with an inscription written by himself, but
whether his body lies here is a question that can
never be definitely answered.

Beyond Battersea Bridge is a little creek, and
from a small house on the other side of the road
Turner used to look out upon the river.   He came
here incognito from his real house in Queen Anne
Street, and studied the gorgeous sunset effects,
which can be seen nowhere better than at Chelsea.

CHELSEA REACH WITH THE OLD CHURCH

Now in his palace of the west,
   Sinking to slumber, the bright day,
Like a tired monarch fanned to rest,
   Mid the cool airs of evening lay;
While round his couch's golden rim
   The golden clouds like courtiers crept,
Struggling each other's light to dim,
   And catch his last smile ere he slept.
                    —*Moore.*

Turner brings us to modern memories. Besides himself and Carlyle, there lived in Chelsea, Rossetti and George Eliot, not to mention living men.

Opposite Chelsea is the long wall that bounds Battersea Park, and after passing Battersea Bridge, we encounter a very unlovely strip of water, with wharves and chimneys and tumble-down buildings. It is utilitarian and not beautiful.

The green embankment which hems in the grounds of Hurlingham Club gives a touch of relief, and the fine trees which existed long before the club, since the time that the house was a private mansion, rise towering above it. On the other side the river Wandle, from which Wandsworth takes its name, a river known to few, empties itself into the Thames. Then we reach Putney Bridge, with its wide, curved white arches. On the east is another embankment which bounds Bishop's Park, partly turned into pleasure gardens

open to all the world.   The palace itself is not well
seen from the river, for it is low and hidden by
trees.

The manor of Fulham has belonged to the See
of London since the end of the seventh century.
The palace is built round two courtyards, the
older of which dates from Henry VII.'s reign,
and the other from the middle of the eighteenth
century.   The west or river side contains the rooms
used by Laud while he was bishop.

As we draw away from the bridge we see to
advantage the two churches, curiously alike, one
belonging to Putney and the other to Fulham,
which stand at two corners of the bridge, diagonally,
looking at one another.   Boat-houses and flats fill
up the western shore until they are succeeded by
the trees of Barn Elms Park, otherwise known as
Ranelagh.   The chief memories of Ranelagh centre
about the Kit-Kat Club, which met here, and
included among the members such men as Walpole,
Vanbrugh, Congreve, Addison and Steele.   Their
portraits were all painted by Sir Godfrey Kneller,
and hung round the club room; consequently, this
particular size of portrait, 36 inches by 28, became
known as a kit-kat.   The name of the club itself
is said to have originated in a pastrycook named

Christopher Kat, who used to make excellent mutton pies, called Kit-Kats, which were always included in the bill of fare at club dinners.

Many a visit did Evelyn and Pepys and other notable Londoners make to Barn Elms in summer evenings in the seventeenth century. Pepys was particularly fond of idling under the well-grown trees. Hear him:

> After dinner, by water, the day being mighty pleasant, and the tide serving finely, I up as high as Barne Elmes and there took one turn alone.

This was in April; and another time:

> I walked the length of the Elmes, and with great pleasure saw some gallant ladies and people come with their bottles and baskets and chairs, to sup under the trees by the water-side, which was mighty pleasant.

On the opposite side of the river from Barn Elms stood Brandenburg House, where lived Queen Caroline, unhappy consort of George IV.

Below Hammersmith Bridge there is a very untidy bit of foreshore, with factories and chimneys and many dreary objects scattered about it, and always a superfluity of clumsy barges. Beyond the fine suspension bridge there is another bit of foreshore not quite so untidy, where racing boats and other boats lie, and from which many a crew turns out to practice. Along this stretch runs the

25

Mall, Upper and Lower. In the coffee house near the junction of the two, Thomson wrote " Winter," in *The Seasons*.

The Mall is associated with the Kelmscott Press, founded by William Morris, who named it after his country house. Turner lived in the Mall for six years, and the novelist Marryat was a resident for a short time in 1830. Here also was a large house occupied by Catherine of Braganza after the death of Charles II. The river at Hammersmith is 750 feet wide. The inhabitants make the bridge a favourite lounging place, for seats line both sides ; the total amount of fresh air thus imbibed no man can calculate, for the tide races up bringing ozone straight from the sea, and the wind blows freshly over the glittering water. On the south bank are the reservoirs of a large water company.

With Hammersmith we must end this chapter, for we have joined the account of the stream of pleasure which comes down to London.

CHAPTER XIX

OUR NATIONAL POSSESSION

THE Thames is a great national possession, affording means of recreation and delight to thousands yearly. It is difficult to compare it with anything else in Great Britain. It stands by itself, and is unique. Other rivers there are, which for a small part of their course are excellent for boating; but there is nothing in England to equal the Thames, where the water is now kept at a high level, and where, for the 112 miles between London Bridge and Oxford, there is practically continuous beauty and convenience for boating. The reproach has been brought against us that we do not make full use of our river at London as the Parisians do of the Seine at Paris. But the two things are not on the same footing at all. There are many problems in connection with the Thames as a tidal river that have not to be solved by the Parisians in regard to the Seine. Perhaps if the great barrage at Gravesend, which has been discussed, ever comes into existence, we shall be able to remove the reproach, to run our steamboats to time, and to use the river as a river of pleasure, even so far down as London Bridge. There are, however, grave objections to the barrage scheme, which for the present has been set aside. Though the tides interfere with pleasure boats, they are a source of motive power for innumerable barges; the river traffic would be seriously hindered by the elimination of the element of tide, and many owners of wharves and quays would be injured by the change. There are also other difficulties. At present the sewage, after being dealt with by filtration in sewage-beds, is returned to the river, and, having been rendered innocuous, floats out to sea, and mingles with the pure water satisfactorily. It would, however, be another thing to return thousands of gallons of water, which, however

FROM BATTERSEA BRIDGE

innocuous, can hardly be called clean, to the great lake of fresh water the river would become if dammed up by a barrage.

Yet the continual increase in the size of ships, and the consequent demand for a river ever deeper, is a source of perplexity to the Thames Conservancy. This involves constant dredging, which would not be necessary were a perpetual high tide to be maintained. It is true that this dredging in some parts is a source of profit, not of expense. Thames gravel is exceedingly valuable, and it is found to be worth while for men not only to buy and maintain large dredgers down near the river mouth, but to pay a rent of something like £1500 to the Conservancy for the privilege of doing so! The dredging, however, is not all so profitable. Where the river-bed is slime and mud, the channel has to be kept clear by dredgers at the expense of the Conservancy, and no delightful rents accrue from the process. This dredging is altogether rather an interesting matter. In some places it is found remunerative enough for men to do it by hand for the sake of what they bring up, and they obtain leave to go dredging.

It is a fact not realised by everyone that the whole river, and all the craft upon it are under the

strictest surveillance.   Everything that floats must
be licensed and carry its number for purposes of
ready identification.   The barges seen lying about
in shoals near Westminster or Waterloo Bridges
are not lying haphazard, but in certain specified
places marked by buoys and allotted by the Conservancy, much as cabstands are allotted by the
police.   It is true that quays, wharves, landing
stages, etc., being on land, are not subject to the
Conservancy, which is in the somewhat anomalous
position of dealing with the water, but not with
the banks that hem it in.   Yet the Conservancy
manages to have a finger in this too, for suppose
a man buys a bit of the river's bank, and erects a
boat-building establishment thereon, he is obviously
at a loss without steps down to the water or a
landing place, and for this he has to pay rent to
the Conservancy.   The amusing part of it is that a
man's property is sometimes in the air.   In the case
of a tree growing out of the water, it would truly
tax the judgment of a Solomon to say what the
rights of the Conservancy are toward that tree ; but
it is held that if the tree constitutes any danger or
obstruction to the river-way the Conservators may
insist on its being lopped.   In connection with this
a curious case sometimes arises.   Man is always

cunning where his own interests are concerned. It is not only to one man that the idea has occurred of propping up his overhanging tree by a stake. And, if the stake remains for any length of time, silt and rubbish collect between it and the shore, and eventually the island or the land of the cunning man is enlarged by a foot or two! More; sometimes stakes have been planted in the river bed with the same object without even excuse of the tree. It is the duty of the Conservancy officials to deal with all such stakes.

Whatever may be alleged as to our neglect of the river at London, no such charge can be brought against us in our appreciation of it higher up. Day by day, in the summer, hundreds enjoy the air and the brilliance and the interest of the river reaches. House-boats are moored, permission and licences having been obtained, and men and women practically live in the open air for weeks together. The house-boats are not allowed to anchor everywhere, but are allotted certain stations, due regard being had to the width of the river. If they plant themselves near private ground they must gain the permission of the owner, as well as of the Conservancy, which is quite reasonable.

To preserve an unimpeded channel may be taken

as one of the great duties of the Conservancy. For this reason they have power to remove snags; to prevent the egotistical punt-fisher from placing his punt broadside in the midmost current; and to regulate the rules for the passing of craft. It is rather amusing to see sometimes how the punt man edges his craft as far from the bank as he dare before he sits down on his cane-bottomed chair and sorts out his tackle; but if a Conservancy official come along, and, eyeing him, decides, in spite of his extreme innocency and unconsciousness, that he has encroached too far, back he has to go. It is a perpetual game.

In regard to the fishing, most of the Thames is free; and the coarse fishing—bream, dace, chub, and so on—is good of its kind. Here and there, as at Hedsor, there is a bit preserved. For the commonsense view is taken that, if both banks belong to the same owner, the river bed belongs also to him, and likewise the fishing. He cannot, however, prevent boats from passing up and down the stream flowing through his property, or the highway would be a highway no more. The fishery in the Thames has of late years greatly improved, owing to the disinterested action of many clubs and associations in putting in stock which they cannot hope subsequently to reclaim, but which, once gone into the water, belongs to everyone alike. An instance of this occurred recently, when 300 trout (*Salmo fario*), about fourteen inches long, were put into the Thames at Shepperton Weir in March by the Weybridge, Shepperton, and Halliford Thames Trout Stocking Association. These trout cost 2s. 6d. each! There is good coarse fishing in nearly all parts of the Thames; bream, dace, chub, perch, and pike can generally be caught.

There are many curious and interesting points in regard to the river, and none more interesting than those relating to the tow-path. This venerable and ancient right-of-way still remains, crossing and recrossing from side to side as occasion demands, but traversable from end to end. As, however, it passes through private grounds by far the greater part of the way, it *is* private, and yet public. Bicycles are frequently forbidden by stern notices put up by owners, who yet cannot prevent the pedestrian. The Conservancy has no power over the tow-path. What, then, happens when a part of the tow-path gives way and requires making up again? In theory it is the owner's duty to do it; but it would be expecting rather more than is warranted of human nature to expect an owner, who must regard the right-of-way with dislike and suspicion, to incur expense by mending it. As a matter of fact, if he does not do it, the Conservancy does. It may be remarked here that a very simple and effective way of embanking, known as "camp-shedding," is often employed about the river banks and the projecting points of lock islands which are liable to be carried away by the current. This consists in dropping large bags of dry cement into the water. The water itself consolidates and hardens the stuff, which becomes a splendid barrier.

There is another point in connection with the breaking away of the tow-path which is still more perplexing. Supposing it breaks away from a private owner's land in such a way that it cannot be built up again, but must be carried inland, what right has the public to say, "My right-of-way has fallen into the water, so I am going to take some of your land to replace it"? Apparently none at all. Yet the tow-path must be carried on. One wonders how, in the beginning, it was allotted to one side or the other. How was it that one owner said, "My lawns must slope right down to the water's edge; therefore I will not have the tow-

path on my side; let it go upon the other?"
And why has it never happened that two owners,
equally strong and equally determined, have both
flatly refused it? Be that as it may, the tow-path
runs its tortuous but continuous course, and will
continue to run as long as the river flows.

Such things as locks and weirs are, of course,
entirely in the power of the Conservancy, who pay
the keepers and regulate the fees. The half-tide
lock at Richmond has answered admirably so far
(*see* p. 196); but the question is, Where is this
sort of thing going to stop? There is an idea
now of a similar lock at Wandsworth, and then
we come to the matter of the barrage. We are so
greedy of our river, we want it to be pent up,
and not allowed to flow away to the sea. Weirs
of some sort, which were at first called locks, are
very ancient. In the end of the twelfth century
we find orders respecting them.

Stow tells us that about the year 1578 or 1579
there were twenty-three "locks," sixteen mills,
sixteen floodgates and seven weirs on the river
between Maidenhead and Oxford. In the next
six years thirty more locks and weirs had been
made in spite of complaints that many persons
had been drowned "by these stoppages of the

26

water." He adds that "the going up the locks was so steep that every year cables had been broken that cost £400." Especial complaint was made about Marlow lock, where one man had had his brains dashed out, and Stow remarks that all the compensation the widow received was £5! The barges were not charged for going up but only for coming down, and a barge passing from Oxford to London in Stow's time paid £12 18s. This was in the summer, when the water was low. In 1585 a petition was made to Queen Elizabeth " in the name of the widows and fatherless children whose parents and husbands were by these means slain, against the great mischief done to her loving subjects by the great number of dangerous locks, weirs, mills and floodgates unlawfully erected in many places on the river." Queen Elizabeth must have known something of the subject from her early acquaintance with Bisham. (*See* Chap. XI.)

In an old book of 1770 we find this passage: " The locks were machines of wood placed across the river, and so contrived to hold the water as long as convenient, that is, till the water rises to such a height as to allow of depth enough for the barge to pass over the shallows, which being effected, the water is set at liberty, and the loaded vessel proceeds on its voyage till another shoal requires the same convenience to carry it forward. This arrangement was in the summer when the water was low; in other seasons the locks were removed."

When the present locks were made they were called "pound" locks; a great many of them were opened between 1770 and 1780.

The members of the Conservancy Board go up in their launch several times a year to see that all is in order, and that their officials are doing their duty. Once a year they penetrate beyond Oxford, where the launch cannot go, and they have to take to rowing boats. They are not supposed to preserve the amenities of the river, but only its highway properties. They have no power to remove unsightlinesses, such as hideous advertisement boards; but only obstructions. Yet, in keeping the river free from sewage contamination; by forbidding the casting of refuse into the current from house-boats or elsewhere; by exercising a general jurisdiction, which makes people realise they are not free to amuse themselves to the annoyance of their neighbours—no doubt the amenities are very much more preserved than they would otherwise be.

Stow ends up his account of the river: "And thus, as this fine river is of great use and profit to the city, so the many neat towns and seats on the banks of it make it extraordinary pleasant and delightful. So that the citizens and gentlemen, nay kings, have in the summer time usually taken the air by water; being carried in boats and barges along the Thames, both upward and downward according to their pleasures."

INDEX

Printed by GEO. W. JONES, LIMITED, *Watford.*

BEAUTIFUL BOOKS
ILLUSTRATED IN COLOUR
BY MORTIMER MENPES

JAPAN WITH 100 FULL-PAGE ILLUSTRATIONS IN COLOUR PRICE **20s.** NET	**The Times.**—"Mr. Menpes's pictures are here given in most perfect facsimile, and they form altogether a series of colour impressions of Japan which may fairly be called unrivalled. Even without the narrative they would show that Mr. Menpes is an enthusiast for Japan, her art and her people; and very few European artists have succeeded in giving such complete expression to an admiration in which all share."
INDIA WITH 75 FULL-PAGE ILLUSTRATIONS IN COLOUR PRICE **20s.** NET	**The Evening Standard.**—"This sumptuous book is the result of an ideal collaboration, for the artist is at his best with colour schemes and atmospheric impressions, such as we find in his famous 'Japan' and 'Durbar' books; while Mrs. Steel has not only the saving grace of imagination, but is able by the sympathy and wise knowledge gained by a long residence in India to write a text of more than ordinary charm."
THE DURBAR WITH 100 FULL-PAGE ILLUSTRATIONS IN COLOUR PRICE **20s.** NET	**Morning Post.**—"This splendid book will be accepted by all as the best realisation of an epoch-making ceremony that we are ever likely to get." **The Academy.**—"Unquestionably the best pictorial representation of the Durbar which has appeared." **The Globe.**—"Likely to be the most brilliant and lasting record of the historical occasion."
VENICE WITH 100 FULL-PAGE ILLUSTRATIONS IN COLOUR PRICE **20s.** NET	**The King.**—"Within the last few years the industry of contemporary writers, some with and others without a genuine sympathy for their subject, has helped us to glimpses of the Queen of the Adriatic, through the spectacles of art, history, archæology, poetry, and romance; but the *Magnum Opus* of Mortimer Menpes embraces to a great degree all five points of view, and persuades us that at last (and that not a day too soon) the stones of Venice have found at once a painter and a writer equally worthy of the vanished glories, the memories of which still cling to every church, palace, or bridge drawn or described in this charming work."
BRITTANY WITH 75 FULL-PAGE ILLUSTRATIONS IN COLOUR PRICE **20s.** NET	**Pall Mall Gazette.**—"It is of course the picturesque aspects of Brittany that appeal to Mr. Menpes . . . Whether he paints cottage interiors or peasant types, straggling village streets and coast-town alleys, or a market-place bustling and baking in the sunshine, it is all one to his graceful pencil; and reproduced, as the drawings are, by his own colour-process, they make another of those many charming albums of travel which Messrs. Black have made a special province of their own."

PUBLISHED BY ADAM AND CHARLES BLACK · SOHO SQUARE · LONDON · W.

Lightning Source UK Ltd.
Milton Keynes UK
UKOW041808241111

182637UK00006B/19/P